The Possur

LHP

Advance Praise For Aunt Eloise and The Possum That Crossed The Road...

"Raise your hand if you knew the real identity of Aunt Eloise all these years...uhmm...yeah, sure. Toby is a 'man's man' but knows just enough about how women think to have pulled off this great prank for years. Now that you know 'who' she is, does it make you re-think all those times when she was just a sweet old lady? Or...is he a 'she' pretending to be a 'he' coming out as a 'she'? One thing's for sure...Aunt Eloise will always keep us guessing...and laughing!"

--Cathy Martindale, zMac Racing Country and WSM-FM, Nashville.

" I remember driving south toward Memphis in the early 80's and just above the Tennessee border in southwest Kentucky, I picked up WMC 79 and began listening to Aunt Eloise just before the 'Incredible 8:10'...(a feature that gave listeners one joke after another for an extended period of time.)....so the feature comes on and I'm laughing...laughing so hard I had to pull over to the side of the road...all the while loving what I was hearing...and all of this and then some because Les Acree had the good sense to hire Aunt Eloise many years before.. It is a moment in time permanently written in my mind...Thank you. Eloise!"

–Jay Phillips, owner KLBQ-FM and KDMS-AM in El Dorado, Arkansas

"I met Toby in Memphis in the late 1970s, and it was like running into your best friend from High School, even though we had never met. He was a breath of fresh air to the Memphis Radio Market."

-- Larry Rogers, Record Producer and Owner of Studio 19, Nashville, Tennessee

"We first meet thru NASCAR Races, and I was a big fan of the radio show. After the races on Sunday, he would interview the winning drivers on the radio Monday morning and I just fell in love with Aunt Eloise. To be so convincing with all the people he played on the radio takes a great talent. We have been close friends for the last 25 years.He is an honest and down to Earth person and God has truly blessed him.I love Toby very much."

--Flossie Johnson the First Lady of NASCAR.

The official caterer for reading this book is Pulliams Hot Dogs, 4400 Old Walkertown Rd, Winston-Salem, NC 27105, Mark Flynt, CEO.

"Eat More Possum"

The Possum That Crossed The Road

My Life As Aunt Eloise

By Robert Thomas Young

With Thomas D. Perry

Copyright 2014 Robert Thomas Young and Thomas D. Perry

ISBN-13: 978-1500376550

ISBN-10: 1500376558

Tom Perry's Laurel Hill Publishing LLC
P. O. Box 11
4443 Ararat Highway
Ararat, VA 24053
www.freestateofpatrick.com
freestateofpatrick@yahoo.com
276-692-5300

Title page photograph of transistor radio won by Toby Young from WCOS in Columbia, South Carolina, at age 12 along with photos of his grandmother's Elise and Louise, who became the basis for Aunt Eloise and finally the CMA DJ of the Year Award.

Cover page photograph of Aunt Eloise caricature from the days at WTQ in Winston-Salem, North Carolina.

TOM PERRY'S LAUREL HILL PUBLISHING LLC

WWW.FREESTATEOFPATRICK.COM

Toby would like to dedicate this book to his wife, Tammy, their daughters, Tabitha, and Tara, and his parents, Jim and Frieda Young.

Tom would like to dedicate this book to Reid and Sadie Smith, their four sons: Ricky, Joey, Davey, and Greg along with their families, big fans of Aunt Eloise in Ararat, Virginia.

Note To The Reader

This book is based on the writings of Robert Thomas "Toby" Young along with interviews conducted by Thomas D. Perry during 2014. This work is autobiographical in nature and is based on memory. The authors have made every effort to tell this story correctly, but with works of this nature, mistakes occur and for that, we apologize.

Well, not really. Get over yourself. It is a book with possum in the title. I mean, really! ☺

Please place your tongue firmly in your cheek while reading thi massive tome of literature!

All errors are the sole responsibility of the Robert Thomas "Toby" Young and not the publisher.

Contents

The Possum That Crossed The Road	11
Possum Photo Album	137
A Few Words From the Ghost Writer In The Sky	191
Acknowledgements	195
Index	197

Toby and Tammy Young with a cutout of Aunt Eloise Louise Cotton.

Chapter One

In the spring of 1865, William T. Sherman's United States Army made its way to Columbia, South Carolina, where it began an urban renewal project that my "Ghost Writer" tells me was to make the state pay for starting the War of Northern Aggression, War Between the States, War for Southern Independence, or the most UN-Civil War in history. Some of Sherman's "Bummers" made their way to the Cotton Family's farm on the outskirts of Columbia, where they encountered the family mule. When one of the "Yankees" decided to mount the beast, he quickly found out the animal had Southern tendencies and the mule deposited him on his backside. The angry "Yankee" shot the mule ending the Cotton Family's fighting in what Scarlett O'Hara called the "War! War! War!"

Thus begins my story with the war that all Southerners like to talk about and one of my grandparent's families, who had the great Southern name of Cotton. This is my story and how I became Aunt Eloise Louise Cotton on the radio for many decades.

I am ready to write a book about the true stories about Aunt Eloise Louise Cotton. The story you are about to read is true. I changed some names to protect the guilty. I was born in November 1955, third of three brothers, the baby brother, in Eastover, South Carolina. My brothers have reminded me of that all my life.

Until I was three or four years old, we lived in Columbia, South Carolina, next to my mother's parents. My brothers and I called Alvin B. Taylor, a well-respected contractor, and his wife, Louise, City Grandpa and City Grandma.

My father, James H Young Jr., entered the National Guard. We moved to the country about a mile from my father's parents and eighteen miles from the city of Columbia.

My Pop's parents were James H. Young and Elise Cotton Young. Everybody in Lower Richland County, South Carolina, knew "Jim H." As a farmer, he grew cotton, peaches, watermelon, cantaloupe, winter wheat, and later soybeans.

My grandmother was a good farmer herself. She grew a garden that was at least two acres big. If you could plant it, she grew it. Among these were butter beans (my favorite), tomatoes, peppers, squash, pole beans, corn, and strawberries.

She had a little white stand Granddaddy would set up by the highway to sell peaches. As kids, my brothers and I would sell watermelons off the back of a truck. If you ever went to Myrtle Beach through Columbia on Highway 76, the Garner's Ferry Road, to Sumter, South Carolina, in the late 1950s and the 1960s, you could have stopped and bought some peaches from my grandma or a cantaloupe and watermelon from me.

My parents were strict in a good way that today would not be "politically correct." My brothers and I got "whoopings." If we cussed, we got our mouths washed out with soap. My parents wanted a girl and they got one eventually in Aunt Eloise.

We grew up hunting and fishing on the farm. I think you learn about life quicker on a farm than in the city. You learn about the cycles of life, birth and death, and you appreciate your air-conditioned job in a radio station a whole lot better. Today, my Daddy still fishes at 88 years old.

It was hot and dirty work on the farm. We grew a lot of soybeans in South Carolina. In October/November, you used the combine, dropped them into the truck, and carried them to the market near Orangeburg while listening to Clemson Football on the radio.

In the winter, it was winter wheat, but you did not farm much and then the holidays came with Thanksgiving and Christmas. Momma always had a Christmas Club at the bank, where she put aside $10 a week.

On Christmas Day, Bo and Daddy went hunting with their coon dogs for...gulp...possums. Being the youngest, I helped Momma in the kitchen. At Thanksgiving, we watched Macy's parade. At Christmas In the afternoon, we watched the Blue-Grey Football Game, where the best players from teams not going to bowl games played.

Daddy had an "Earth Station." What we call today a satellite dish, but it was a big one, what some people call the "West Virginia State Flower," which rotated. We could watch game feeds and hear all the comments that did not make it to television broadcasts such as the cameramen focusing on well-endowed young ladies in the stands, risqué comments by the announcers, or the coaches cussing. Well, the the dishes were scrambled and you had to pay for codes to activate them and later you paid for codes for each channel. It became too much to keep up with, but today we have the smaller versions packaged together.

We played sports and my older brothers excelled at them whether it was football, baseball, and basketball. My oldest brother Bo and middle brother Danny played at Lower Richland High School including state championships in 1971-72. I still remember seeing them on television.

I always thought the idea that women were not passionate about sports was wrong. My mother played and the women in my family were and are just as excited about college football, whether it was Clemson and now, yes, even the University of South Carolina.

My family has become divided between Tigers and Gamecocks fans. We were once Clemson Tiger fans and now a disease inspired by "The Old Ball Coach," Steve Spurrier, has infected my family. During my absences a new generation was born. Every year Momma gave out presents mostly from Clemson and now more and more from the South Carolina Gamecocks. Over the years, I noticed something had happened to my family. Now, there is tension every year during the holidays, but no fights. It is all in good fun. I can remember seeing my nephew, who is a trainer at USC working in sports medicine carrying the "enemy" off the field. There have even been Georgia Bulldogs marry into my family. How did this happen? As I write this, Clemson has not beat USC in football in a long time, but I am keeping hope alive.

In the spring when Easter came around, off to Columbia, we went to buy new clothes for church. My mother liked to invade our personal space. She would pick up a napkin, lick it, and wipe off our faces when needed.

On Sundays, there was no fishing or playing cards. We were Christian people. We went to church, but I hated that tie and suit. Life revolved around the church including hayrides. We went to the Methodist Church and had a deep belief in Jesus. There were many good people who influenced us.

Beulah Baptist and Lebanon Methodist congregated together. There were all sorts of jokes about this such as you can always tell a Methodist because they always brought a covered dish, while a Baptist would go to the liquor store, but they would not dance. Methodist could only afford a piano, while those rich Baptists could afford an organ. The two groups alternated weeks. Every summer, there was Vacation Bible School.

My father was tough at times, but he showed his love. When I wrecked on my first date with my first love, Cindy, I thought he was going to be mad, but he hugged me and told me not to worry. Like the prodigal son, I was scared he was going to get me. Later, he was not so forgiving. I think it scarred him as much as it did me.

You never disrespected women. When my mother put food on the table, you ate it or you did not eat. We were just country people living a simple life.

Daddy was in the Air National Guard. I remember during the Cuban Missile Crisis in October 1962, things were tense. He worked on jets as a Master Sergeant, but he was on alert 24/7.

When you visited him at the base, there were certain lines you did not cross. One yellow line comes to mind when I crossed it he said, "Son Back Up! Don't ever cross that line." It was serious stuff and serious times.

Back then, Daddy was at Congaree Air Force Base, now McIntyre Air Base. I can remember him flying with Strom Thurmond or Fritz Holland, both Governors and U. S. Senators from South Carolina. He flew on a prop engine plane we called a "Gooney Bird." I remember seeing the ramp come down and my Daddy walking with Strom Thurmond. I thought "Strom knows my Dad."

Your foundation begins in youth and stays with you when you are older. Daddy ran an Officer's Club at the Air Base. There was a kid's room off the main club and I often went in there to watch television. I thought there were three great voices in music: George Jones, Elvis, and

Tom Jones. At age eleven or twelve there I was watching Tom Jones on a television on the wall. Years later, Tom Jones came to Nashville to record some country songs for Mercury Records and I got to meet him.

A Black comedian, named of all things George Wallace, opened for Tom Jones. Wallace liked to say, "Don't tell me no jokes." Backstage with Jones and Wallace I said to George, "I got a joke for you." He just went crazy, but I told him, "What do you call a White man on a bus with eleven Black guys?...Coach." George cracked up laughing at me. You might not remember that many singers like Elvis had comedians open their shows for them.

Growing up in South Carolina, we were Explorer Scouts and we got into some trouble on the Air Force Base and nearby Fort Jackson. Military Police did not like it when you threw clothes into jet engines. They also did not like it when you rode dirt bikes across fields where mortars, grenades, and bombs might lay unexploded. They told us we might want to ride elsewhere.

The South Carolina Highway Patrol did not like our dirt bikes on public highways such as Highway 76. Dirt bikes were great for jumping and we would find some great woods and sand cliffs to explore, but when crossing the state road, the troopers were waiting for us often. I hid in the woods and the trooper would get on the loud speaker saying, "Alright Toby, I know you are in there." It was like living in *Smokey and the Bandit*. I waited the trooper out and kept close to the side of the road on the way home in case I needed to escape to the safety of the woods again.

We often found ourselves at the old Cotton Plantation. It was falling in on itself, but I remember it had this great spiral staircase. Once Bo and I shot at a man who worked for Daddy with BB guns from an upstairs window. The man thought bees were stinging him, but Daddy was not amused and we got a "whupping." We played "War of Northern Aggression" with bottle rocket fights, but nobody wanted to be on the "Yankee" side.

I appreciate home more living away from it as I have these many decades. When my favorite dog, Ressie Star Young, died I took her home to my land near Eastover, South Carolina, where I am going to retire, to bury her, so she would be close to me. I always think of that Joe South song "Don't it make you wanna go home." I parodied that song once along with others such as Bobby Sue of the Oak Ridge Boys for the "Light, Gas and Robbery."

Chapter Two

Once I heard that WCOS, the AM radio station in Columbia, South Carolina, was having a Slurpee Contest based on the 7-11 drink, where you called in to guess which DJ could drink or slurp it down the fastest. It got hot in South Carolina, so a Slurpee was a good thing. I called in and to my amazement, I got on the air and was terrified. I won a transistor radio that I still have to this day. I loved Hunter Herring. He played the soundtrack of my youth at Lower Richard High School. My Granddaddy took me over to the radio station to get the radio. Little did I know that one day, I would be working there with my hero Hunter Herring.

I remember WCOS had a promotion at a gas station near my City Grandparents. I came by on my bike to watch. The DJ asked me what to play, and I suggested the song "Classical Gas," an instrumental tune popular at the time.

The DJ told me I should be on the radio. I went home and started mimicking him at twelve years old.

We had a Ham Radio Station at home near the farm and eventually a tower in the backyard. I had a utility closet off the carport where I talked on the CB radio to my City Granddaddy.

I remember a friend, Tommy Thomason, the redheaded son of local furniture dealer, who banged a drum, saying he was drumming up business for my daddy. Those were the days growing up in and near Columbia.

Growing up in South Carolina at that time, there were a hand full of things that I looked forward to every year after I turned twelve. Among these were the Southern 500 in Darlington, Clemson/South Carolina football game, The Masters in Augusta, and the first week at the beach. Not necessarily in that order.

Now before I was twelve at the end of school year, I would go stay in Columbia with my City Grandparents in the summer for a few weeks. City Granddaddy was a big ham radio operator and had his own radio station in a little workshop by his garage. He even had a tower with a rotor antenna he could move 360 degrees. Now this caused mo than one neighbor to get upset with City Granddaddy when on Saturda nights folks would tune in their TV sets to hear "One Adam 12 One Adam 12 Code 5 Hollywood And Vine" and instead heard "10 4 Good Buddy This Is KSL 3587 A.B. Taylor Calling From The Capital City Of Columbia South Carolina. You Got A Copy BG. How Are Things in Arizo BG?" That BG was Senator Barry Goldwater of Arizona, but that did no mean a thing to me or the neighbors, who wanted to hear Officer Pete Malloy and not A.B. Taylor.

I loved those summer nights listening and talking to folks. The radio bug bit me big time. I loved going to work with "Mister AB" as everybody called him. He built a few houses at the same time and he inspected the work to make sure everything was going right. Later, he became an inspector for building construction for Columbia.

My City Grandma was a funny and feisty woman. She always complained about the crooked politicians and how the power company was raising the power rates. She never missed a chance to say what she thought, even to me. Louise stood her ground and if she thought the meter reader stepped on her flowers, she would have a new flower planted and paid for by South Carolina Electric and Gas.

She was a good cook too. One summer after riding my bike all over Columbia, I came in for lunch and she surprised me with a double cheeseburger she called "The Big Lou." After fixing the burger, she toasted it in the oven and oh, that crunchy sound and the taste of the cheese was so good. I loved City Grandma and Grandpa so much and they had a lot to do with shaping my future.

Back on the farm, my brother, Bo, rigged up a radio with a pair of headsets so we could listen to the radio when plowing or cultivating with that old John Deere tractor.

Now I discovered girls at twelve and from then on, I hated the farm. I used to have to pull weeds by hand in the Soybean fields because the tractor never got them all and the weed killers were not 100% effective. My family called me "Tobycide," a weed's worst enemy. Many a Friday afternoon or Saturday afternoon, I would be on that John Deere plowing up a 90-acre field and I had that radio blasting through the headsets.

Working with Country Granddaddy on the farm was a lesson in life. He had a great sense of humor and sang in the church. Every night before going to bed, he read a chapter from the Bible. He sang at weddings and everybody loved "Mr. Jim H."

He helped build the old Cooper River Bridge in Charleston, South Carolina. The crew lived on Pawley's Island in a boarding house where my Country Grandmother was the cook. The crew took a barge each day after she fed about twenty men and, of course, fixed sandwiches for lunch and had supper ready when they got off work. Elise Cotton Young, until the day she died, always cooked like that.

After Country Granddaddy died, I went to live with her. I

remember his funeral because there were cars parked all over the highway and our church only held about 250 people. There were folks standing outside, hundreds of folks, Black and White. All folks respected my Country Granddaddy because he treated everybody equal. I cry when I hear that the White folks in the south hated Black folks because that is a lie. My Grandfather was a man who cared for all people.

Now I said Country Grandmother cooked. Although it was just she and I, she had enough food to feed twenty. Many of my friends knew this and sometimes we had almost twenty folks coming to eat.

I was about 13 at the time, and yes, I had girls on my mind, but living with her was sad sometimes because she missed granddaddy after he passed. They were married for over fifty years and she would cry. I am sure the Good Lord helped me make her laugh. I did know what to do. It made me sad, but just like a lightning strike I started talking to her in what is now Aunt Eloise speak. She burst out laughing when I would talk about cooking possum and telling jokes as Eloise. I am glad to say that three of my Grandparents lived to see my success in radio. I am glad because there was a lot of all four of them in Aunt Eloise Louise.

Chapter Three

In a scene that could have come from Lake Woebegone, Daddy and I had a "Honey Tank" explosion. We were draining the cow manure from the cow barn when the hose busted. Daddy was on the tractor running the power take off and I at age 14 or 15 was near the tank. We found ourselves covered from head to toe. We had to drive the tank to the farm by Bunky Carter's Store and if seen, we would never hear the end of it. Well, if it could not have gotten worse, we met Carter on the road. He was pointing his finger at us. We heard about it for a very long time. We ended up naked in the yard at home hosing each other off before we could go in the house.

I had a summer job on a cousin's aunt's golf course, which was the worst golf course in the world. We parked golf carts, caddied, dove in ponds for golf balls, and sold hot dogs. The Twilight Drive In movie theater nearby gave us an opportunity to play a practical joke. We told guys at the theater there was a lady who was a nymphomaniac. Her husband was out of town and she would be at the golf course. Guys arrived and we flashed car lights and told them she was just over the hill waiting on a green with a sleeping bag waiting for them when suddenly a guy with a shotgun appeared pretending to be the angry husband shooting into the sky. Some of the guys ran a mile down to the nearby highway and told the highway patrol there was a crazy man trying to kill people. One summer we did it five or six times and none of the guys admitted to it so it worked repeatedly with other guys.

The head football coach at Lower Richland High School once told me that I was the greatest tackle dummy he ever coached. Thus, my career as a football star ended.

Instead, I drove the school bus. I had the longest bus route in the state of South Carolina. I bring up the bus because I have an interesting story to tell about the first and only race riot that I witnessed.

Integration came to South Carolina when I entered the 4th grade circa 1965. Living in Lower Richland County, we were country folks. I knew many Black kids growing up. We played together or worked on the farm with each other. We had our moments, but by and by, it seemed to be more of a problem for the people from the city.

My bus was 95% Black and they were all my friends. We rode home on the afternoon ride singing together all the songs we heard on the radio. From The Four Tops "Ain't To Proud To Beg" to "Proud Mary". We had a good time. Then one day in shop class, we heard a rumor that some kids from Columbia were coming down to start a riot. We had one break out in the lunchroom. People were running all over the place and I remember picking up a welding rod, when a teacher told me to put it down.

Over the PA, we heard the Principal say, "Bus drivers go to your buses, and students go to your bus or cars. School is dismissing." I took off to my bus after making sure my girlfriend got to her car and left.

When I got to the bus lot, I saw my bus and it was full. The other buses had a few standing around, but my bus was full. I was the rural bus driver remember. All my kids were country and farm folks. Well I heard Willamette, a bus rider, yell, "Toby get us out of here; them city Negroes is crazy." I jumped on board, counted heads, and I was gone.

Can you believe they came to our school to start a fight? Willamette Scott started taking about "Red Fern," a bad Black man, who started it .The fear on their faces scared me to death. I will never forget that moment in my life. Those kids just wanted an education and no trouble. We did not sing that day.

Back on that John Deere again with the radio blasting, I was listening to WCOS's Hunter Herring, The Boogie Man. The 1960s were a great time for DJs. They made the music exciting and Hunter Herring made that radio bug bite me again. He was the 6 p.m. to 10 p.m. Disc Jockey that everybody listened to while getting showered and dressed to chase the women in Columbia. Listening to this funny and energetic man got you in the groove, as we once said. I thought I want to do that for a living. He was the guy MCing the Big Mini Skirt or Bikini Contest. He was so cool and hip. Man, I really hated the farm now.

My City Grandfather helped me purchase a Mustang for $1,500. I put blue shag carpet in it to go with the 8-Track tape player. In South Carolina, after they changed the legal drinking age from eighteen to twenty-one, we all started going to the drive-in movie.

After losing my first true love in high school my junior year, my senior year was no better. I lost my driver's license and my job as a school bus driver. I lost my license because of an accident driving the bus in an intersection that I could not see well. I eased the bus out and car clipped it; a state owned car driven by two ladies from Clemson.

My friend, Jarred O'Neal, picked me up at my grandmother's to get me to school and afterwards, I thumbed a ride home. I never drove again after I wrecked my Mustang. I did get the part in the play that Andy Griffith had in *No Time For Sergeants* my last year in the high school.

I got a part time job at WCOS right before my break up junior year. I ran the Sunday morning shows and got a five-minute newscast once a morning. I ran American Top Forty, but after graduation, I had to "Get the hell out of Dodge."

I was seventeen years old at the beach living the dream. I did have a disturbing experience about this time. I hitchhiked, as I could not drive to get to school or to the beach. My mom drove me, but in the afternoons, I could either wait for her or thumb a ride home.

This bald headed creepy fellow, who said he worked at a Baptist Bookstore, picked me up and gave me a ride. When I graduated, he gave me an envelope with $50 in it. When I protested, he said he liked to help young boys. I should have known better, but it was a different time back then. The word pedophile was not something anybody thought about at that time. Well, I found myself thumbing to the beach after graduation and lo and behold, he picked me saying he was going to the beach too. He offered to let me stay at his place and when he started talking about making my prostate feel good, I asked to get out in Turbeville, saying I had an aunt there I wanted to visit. I went in a diner for a cheeseburger and tried to tell two cops about it, but they were not interested in anything, but lunch. A truck driver overheard my conversation and offered me a ride to the beach where we talked football. I felt much more comfortable.

I went to Myrtle Beach as a Life Guard from 8 a.m. to 5 p.m. on the beach and got a job spinning records at the Castaways on the Strand, The Home Church for Rock And Roll from 7 p.m. to 12 a.m. Another three hours at the afterhour's joints and about four hours sleep before the beach. In order to get over a lost love, I tried more girls. After those summer days at the beach, in the fall it was back to the University of South Carolina and back on the radio at WCOS.

Chapter Four

"We Don't Teach Disc Jockeys." That is what my college professor said my first day in class after asking if anybody had any radio experience. Flash forward after three more radio jobs in Columbia, my third year at USC and summer time came calling me.

I was a big Jimmy Buffet fan after I heard his A1A Album. He was dating a girl named Jane that I met at the Twilight Lounge on Rosewood Drive, a hang out in Columbia for Carolina (USC) students. When I was 16, working at WCOS, the manager David Adams at the Twilight asked me to check IDs, a DJ checking IDs. Eighteen was the drinking age back then, but I was on the radio. No one carded me to purchase alcohol in my life until I was 26 years old, when I bought a drink at the Peach Bowl, a Clemson vs. Kentucky football game. I even kissed the girl who carded me. She said, "Wow! Most of the time I get cussed out." We laughed.

Well, the last song I played at WNOK was Jimmy's *Changes in Latitude*. I told the boss I quit and back to the Castaways at the Beach, I went. Summers always end and this time I moved to Salisbury, North Carolina, to help run a disco for Randy Zimmerson. He wanted to open a club in Columbia. I knew everybody, so back home I went. We opened the Thunderbird Lounge in St Andrews. I worked at the club in the

Thunderbird Motel. I worked with Randy Zimmerson in clubs in Salisbury, North Carolina, who later operated some Gentlemen's Clubs. Working at these clubs exposed me to the good and bad of the business. These clubs did not last long usually. Managing the acts was good, but you could find yourself in some interesting situations. We had The Tams, Sister Rose, and The Drifters. You name a beach band, we had them. Flash forward and I am at WCAY-AM radio in West Columbia and that is where Aunt Eloise debuted.

Back in Columbia at a daytime country music station and spinning records at Big Daddy's Saloon, where "Disco Lives," in the evenings. I started doing a character on my radio show. Eloise was her name and she would come in and cook possum and goats. I used the sound effects from chain saws to goats to drills. Anything I could think off to enhance her cooking. I thought it was funny, but most folks at the station thought I was nuts.

Then one Christmas Eve, the owner came down to the studio. He and his wife lived upstairs, we shut down at sundown, and after I signed off the air, he came in the studio and said, "I cannot pay you what I owe you. Will 50 bucks get you through?" I had heard he was going through tough times, so I took the $50 and bought my Mother some candy, filled my car up, and drove home for Christmas.

WCAY was sold and I got a couple of months work before I lost the job. Today, the call letters WCAY belong to a station in Nashville. WCOS called and they need an all night guy. I took that job quicker than a monkey grabs a banana. I could go back to school, get my degree, and mom will be happy. As ESPN'S Lee Corso would say, "Not So Fast My Friend." I fell in love again and shacked up working the nightclubs and radio again, but all that fell apart and back to the beach, I went.

This time I ran a seafood store in Surfside Beach next to the Holiday Inn. The owners took off a summer to go abroad and their kids came down and took things over, but kept me working at the store.

Then one day, the owners came back and accused me of not picking up an order of three thousand dollars in seafood. I told them that their son was running things. He just told me to mind the store and he took over the books. They believed their son and not me. Although I never wrote a check for anything that summer, his son did, but I got the blame. I drove down to the beach that night and prayed to GOD to help me find an answer to my life.

I went back home to live and my folks were not going to let me sit around and do nothing. I love them for their tough love. After about two weeks of being home, Daddy woke me up and said, "Son, get a job. Me and your mother will do all we can to help you, but you need to take care of yourself." I finally got tired of feeling sorry for myself. I had to do what Pop said.

I got my Federal Communication Commission Ticket. In those days, you had to know how a radio station worked and how to fix it. The test was so hard that some folks complained until the FCC dropped the requirements. A full year later, I finally passed the test.

Once I did the Christmas parade for cable television on Eastover, Richland County, South Carolina, except they did not hold a parade. They needed filler for the cable station, so I got a camera man and went out to the town where there was the post office, liquor store, mini-mart affectionately known as the "Stop and Rob," laundromat, restaurant, and the cotton gin, which really was a cotton gin that sold grain feed, salt blocks, dog food and soybeans. It was a place that showed old Tarzan movies on the side of building to an audience that was 99% African-American.

The cameraman and I stood on the side of the road and I began the narration. A logging truck rolls by and I start talking about how you have to start with the logging industry here in Eastover. Here came a farmer on a tractor representing the agriculture of the region and even a load of hogs made the Christmas parade. People in cars went by waving to the camera. We even had a funeral come by, then there was a milk truck, Coke truck, Budweiser truck, Police and even the Highway Patrol made the parade. We had Miss Eastover when a group of old ladies in a car drove by. At the end, after four hours, Jimmy Christmas, who had a big white beard was Santa.

I got back on at WCOS, my old mentor, Hunter Herring, was doing the morning show, and I was the all night disc jockey again. Before I would leave in the morning, I knew Hunter took phone calls, so from the production room across from the broadcast booth, I called Hunter and ducked down behind the console, and talked to him as Aunt Eloise. He answered and I would say, "Good Morning! Good Morning! Good Morning Hunter, it is Your Aunt Eloise" He would laugh and say, "Well How You Doing Aunt Eloise?" I would go into a funny story about Uncle Tomain hunting possums or start ragging on the power company for raising the rates or the politicians for raising taxes. It was great radio.

After a few weeks, Hunter was telling everybody at the station, "Did you hear Aunt Eloise this morning?" The FM Country jocks were talking about how funny that would be and I just grinned, and thought Toby you might have a good thing here. Well, one day while I was on the air with Hunter, I stood up in the production room where Hunter could see me and when he realized it was me, he busted out laughing. To this day, we are still the best of friends.

Greensboro News and Record Lifestyle section circa 1996.

Chapter Five

Many people on Facebook have asked me if there will be any "sexy" or "juicy" stories in this book. Well, here is the response for all you looking for some sinful stories. When my country grandma cooked, I saw the golden brown delicious, beautiful, sexy fried chicken next to a juicy bowl of gravy. With one sinful eye, I saw the mashed potatoes and collard greens. I felt an evil streak in my body and the food tasted as good as it went down, slowly down to my waiting stomach. YUM!

A couple more great stories out of Columbia. Hardees was the first fast food company to go in to the breakfast business. The folks at Hardees started to bring us the new breakfast biscuits to the morning show. Their steak biscuits were my favorite. Up North, they never heard of a biscuit and since Hardees was only in the South that was soon to change big time. We held a promotion in the WCOS parking lot, where people could drive in, get a free biscuit and cup of coffee, if we could put a WCOS bumper sticker on their car. It was so big we had to have the city's police officers direct traffic. Something the city of Columbia was not crazy about and a few other folks going to work. We backed up traffic and could not do it again. Hardees loved it. We loved it because we had put our bumper sticker on hundreds of cars.

Now, not long after this every other fast food chain went into the breakfast business and the North got their first taste of a sausage biscuit. I am not saying that our promotion that day started the craze that got plenty of local TV, but I am sure other food operators heard about the crowds and who knows, we might have had a little to do with creating the McMuffin.

In Columbia, we once had a contest that had a diamond ring hidden on a statue on the State House grounds. We gave out clues and almost got someone killed when they figured it out and drove too fast getting there to find it.

I was one of the most popular DJs in Columbia in the 1970s doing the morning show on WCOS FM. That was the station we got Aunt Eloise on, but only after this happened. The radio station had the AM and FM studios right across the hall from each other and the AM morning person and the FM morning person were not the best of friends. In fact, they hated each other's guts. I shall call the AM, Dave and the FM, Woody. Now Woody was very popular when I was kid growing up and Dave was a new Program Director from up North, a "Yankee," whose first point of business at the station was to throw out all the beach music. He had no clue how popular beach music was to

South Carolina and just threw them all away to the dismay of the AM and FM staff. Well needless to say, Dave was not very popular, Woody had an ego the size of Myrtle Beach, and the war was on.

One morning after my all night shift on the AM, Rock N Roll, Dave took over to do the morning show and I went back to my apartment for a two-hour nap before my first class at Carolina. Woody came in to do the morning show on FM. Saying good-bye to both I went home only to be woke by our Sales Manager, Jack Grant, on the phone who asked, "Would you please come to station we need you."

I drove the three miles and as I pulled in the parking lot, I saw the city's Chief of Police car and another squad car. I thought, "Oh No! We have been robbed." The station was located downtown Columbia near a street famous for the ladies of the evening. In fact, many of the girls would walk through our parking lot to get to work. I had stood outside the side door during my smoking days and had conversations with them. No, I never had anything, but talk. I thought that maybe one of the women was involved.

I walked into the building and standing next to the men's rest room was Mr. Grant, The Police Chief, our General Manager at the time Jess Plummer, and a couple of officers. My mind was racing. "What is going on? Is there a dead prostitute? Is there a dead Dave or Woody."

After introductions, Mr. Grant said I want you to open the men's room door and tell me what you smell. "Smell?" I asked. "Yes." I opened the door and a strong odor of Marijuana came waffling out. I was asked, "What do you smell?" I turned to Mr. Grant, the Police Chief and said, "I think its marijuana." "Ok tell us what happened last night?" "I don't know. I got off at 6 a.m. and went home." "You know nothing else? "No sir." Well, it was around 8 a.m. and other employees were coming in and were asked what they smelled. Everybody said marijuana.

Then my mentor and radio hero Hunter Herring, The Boggie Man, came walking through. They asked him what he smelled and without a second's hesitation Boogie says, "Man that smells like some Acapulco Gold Ganja, the good stuff." I looked at the Chief, Mr. Grant, and Mr. Plummer and did everything I could not to burst out laughing. The Boss turned red. The police had this stoned look on their faces (no pun intended). Hunter was as serious as he could be.

What happened was Dave went in the bathroom and smelled pot and blamed Woody. They got into verbal battle and Dave called cops. To make a long story short, Dave joined the Columbia Police

Department and actually pulled me over on my way to work, but did not give me a ticket, just a warning. Have no clue to where he is now. Woody remains a DJ today on the air in Columbia and plays lots of beach music. I loved my time in Columbia and worked for Jake Bogan, the only General Manager I ever saw in a Speedo. Jake helped mold Aunt Eloise and taught her a lot about the bizz. Jake is today the President GHB Broadcasting and runs a bunch of stations in the South and one of the oldest Jazz recording studios in the world.

A mentor for me at that time was Joe Pinner, who did the weather at WIS-TV in Columbia. He was popular television icon and gave me some great advice. He was also a hell of a nice guy.

In Columbia, I worked as a DJ at Big Daddy's Saloon at night while doing country radio during the day. I was MC at William Bryce Stadium for concerts, where the Gamecocks play football, where I got to drive on the field. I was DJ at Frat Parties and discovered it became very lucrative.

Early on in my career, I made decisions about what was played on the radio. Here are some stories about that.

In the 1970s, I found myself at dinner with Jerry Weintraub. I did not know he was married to Helen Reddy, who had a hit with "I Am

Woman." She followed it up with "Treat Me Like A Lady." At dinner, I was prompted as to what I thought about it and I said, "I wish she would make up her mind." It did not sit too well with her husband.

Only a few times, did I find "Payola" aimed at me where managers would pay DJs to play their band's music. I always gave it to my General Managers and never played music based on receiving payment to do it.

Some bands were gold such as the Commodores who started with "Machine Gun." I also made mistakes such as thinking that Foghat's "Slow Ride" was not a hit.

I once found myself involved in a controversy about Aerosmith "Walk This Way." The line we played was "Put your kitty in the middle and swing like you didn't care." The sheet music used the word "titty" implying a woman's breasts. A group of ladies complained and came to the radio station. We met with them and played it for them, but they still thought it used the T-word and not the K-word.

Now returning to an ongoing theme of this book...FOOD. Barbeque, as I like, it is from South Carolina and is based on mustard and vinegar and not the tomato based that many of my friends in North Carolina prefer. I believe I should not endorse a product that I do not eat. Historically, the plantation owners in South Carolina ate "high on the hog," which meant they got the good meat from the pig. The slaves got the lower parts of the animal and thus they learned to slow cook it over a fire using mustard as a base.

I think multiculturalism is going to destroy one of the greatest things in the world, ethnic cuisine. A black and white world is dull. I want a Crayola world that includes food from many great ethnic groups. Let people be people. Embrace our differences especially food.

Toby's mentor Les Acree.

Chapter Six

One summer down at the Beach word got out about a band called Alabama that played at The Bowery, a hole in the wall nightclub. It was across from the Pavilion, which has been torn down. You could not get forty people in that place, The Bowery, if they were all greased up with axle grease. They packed that place to hear a bunch of carpenters out of Alabama. Castaways, where I worked, was just about block up from The Bowery.

By day, they tacked carpet and had the crowds in the palm of their hands at night. During band breaks, they put on their carpenter aprons and sold draft beer. They signed a record deal with a label that tried to rip them off, but during all that time, they put out a record, which got some play in Myrtle Beach and my old station WCOS-FM.

We interviewed Randy Owen, Mark Herndon, Jeff Cook, and Teddy Gentry on the morning show a few times before the signing. The band drove up in the morning from the beach to the station in Columbia in a white panel truck with rolls of carpet hanging out the back. They spent a couple hours on the show and drove back to the beach to tack more carpet. It is a good two-hour drive. Then at night, they went back to The Bowery to play until midnight.

Randy's wife, Kelly, came along sometimes. She was a sweetheart. She would drop by, eat lunch, and keep us up to date on the band.

Randy was pretty laid back person as were Jeff and Teddy, but on stage they were like wild party animals. Randy and Teddy jumping all over the stage and Jeff's smoking guitar. He wore a big old gold bass around his neck because he loved fishing. Randy just had that voice that could sing "I Wannna Come Over" with romance dripping from his vocal cords and then cut loose on "Tennessee River" and the party was on.

RCA Records was interested in signing the group and since I had met them, knew the band, and Myrtle Beach, I went with their promotions, Wayne Edwards, to hear the band. Long story short, Alabama signed with RCA.

Wayne Edwards and I became close friends. I could write another book on him. They do not make them like that anymore. He was short, round, long curly, blond hair, cowboy hat, boots, gold chain, leather vest, and cracking jokes all the time, an all around nut.

He played awful or hilarious practical jokes, depending on your sense of humor or lack thereof. On airplanes, he would take cream of mushroom soup and pretend to throw it up in a barf bags and then shock everyone by eating it out of the same bag. He traveled with the African-American country artist Charley Pride and the two of them did some pretty "politically incorrect" things over the years.

When the band did their first concert for RCA it was in Memphis and I just happened to get hired there at WMC 79, so we all got together for the show.

They invited me to come and join the band at their national CMA Award debut. Another DJ, Ron Jordan, tried to expose Aunt Eloise that night at the show. Les Acree took me backstage and threw me into the waiting arms of guess who? Wayne Edwards. The party was on.

The crowds were so big they had to get the band on stage by going through the kitchen door. I do mean the kitchen door. Here I am running with the band, TV cameras and lights chasing us as we ran past the food cooking. Chefs looking at us like nuts. Waiters dodging us and after a few more hallways, left and right turns, we made it backstage.

We all stopped and Wayne caught us in a circle and we all shouted, "Ain't We Having Fun Now" and the guys ran out, grabbed their instruments, and the place went wild. Two songs latter, Wayne lets go, "How do you top that?" For me, a small town person seeing things and people I could not even dream of knowing. The population of

Eastover was about two thousand and half of that was on four legs, but there was a lot coming my way.

Wayne's wife Joanne managed Canadian acts. Whenever you asked her about it, Wayne would start complaining about all those Canadians who want to do is sing about rivers, trees, and beavers.

I found myself in Nashville once with Wayne Edwards when President George H. W. Bush was at the same event, but in another building. Secret Service was everywhere, but Wayne came in a limo through the VIP entrance and did not go through security. Well, Wayne pulls out a Silver 357 Magnum pistol saying, "Look here, Toby." I freaked out telling him to put that gun away. The President of the United States is next door and there is security everywhere.

Chapter Seven

I had the all night show at WCOS-FM and when I got off at 6 a.m., they would let me nap until 7 a.m., and then I would come on the air as Ken Martin's Aunt Eloise Louise Cotton.

My Country Grandmother's name was Elise and my City Grandmother's name was Louise, but for some reason Aunt Elise Louise just did not sink in to the public. The folks would call her Aunt Eloise Louise so that stuck and history is what it is.

The show had great success in just a year and a few months, we were asked to come to Memphis at the only country music station on AM, 5000 watts that was still number because of the FM Boom. Every station on FM was playing what was called elevator music or background. Now they were going Rock or Country. Rick Dees, who was still on AM radio in Memphis, was going to be my competition. In just a year and a half, I am going to Graceland.

At WCOS in Columbia, I first encountered Tammy Dennis. She did not "cotton" to me at first, excuse the pun. I was having a lot of fun with women at the clubs. Tammy was engaged to be married and much more sophisticated than I was. Back then, women dressed in heels, dresses, skirts and you heard them coming down the hall. "Click, click,

click." It took me a year of coaxing to get her go with me to a station promotion. Three months later, we were married and headed to Memphis.

Ken Martin was my first partner as Aunt Eloise in Columbia. We played top 25 country singles and the first two weeks I called in before going to the radio station. After doing Aunt Eloise for a year and a half in Columbia, South Carolina, the brother of radio recruiter Steve Rodney sent him a cassette tape of the character. Les Acree of WMC TV AM FM in Memphis got it and next thing I knew I was on a plane to Memphis to interview for a new job at WMC. The station was located across the street from Woody's, a great place to get a cheeseburger, which was a prerequisite to a radio job.

In 1979, I was married two days after Christmas with a 102 temperature and the flu to Tammy Dennis. My best friend, Ralph Moorer, had picked me up to take me to the church. He told me I looked like I was dying. He laughed saying getting married will make you look that way. We laughed. Today, Ralph and I still stay in touch. Everybody should have a friend like Ralph.

My first day of being married was not the best day. A fellow DJ had by mistake taken my car keys and went to see South Carolina play in the Gator Bowl. We called a locksmith and two hours later and 50 bucks less, we headed to Memphis.

After about twenty minutes, we smelled something bad. My brother had placed anchovies on the manifold of the engine. It could have been worse because we had a Volkswagen and the engine was in the back and it had a convertible top. It was thirty something degrees so after a quick engine wash and we were off again to Memphis. That is when we heard the crickets. Yep, they had put some crickets in the front under the hood and it was time for another wash down. Finally we got to WMC AM FM and TV, all three in the same three story building on Union Avenue.

After finding an apartment and meeting with my new boss and staff, where would you think somebody would want to go in Memphis?...Graceland. At that time, it was not opened to public, but there were some souvenir shops and you could see Graceland from the road. How was I to know that in about two years, I would be doing the first live radio show from the back yard of Graceland with Priscilla Presley and a nine year old Lisa Marie. Before leaving Memphis in 1986, I would get to know all of Elvis's family and friends and have a peanut and banana sandwich made by Mary, the family cook.

"Give Me Information. Give Me Memphis Tennessee." Before we get to Memphis, how about a favorite recipe of mine and we will get back to the book. Grand Dad's Pizza.

You will need one can of Grand Dad's Bisque's. One small can of tomato paste, sausage, ground beef, onions diced, mushrooms chopped, three shredded bags of your favorite cheese, diced green peppers, Pepperonis. Spray a pizza pan with PAM or Butter spray. Take your grands and flatten out the dough on a pizza pan. Smash as flat as you can. Spread mater paste over the dough and spread cheese on top. Next, add all you fixings spreading evenly. Add more cheese. Pre heat oven to 250 degrees, add more cheese, Place in oven for 20 minutes. Make sure the crust is brown before taking it out the oven. When it looks ready, do as the French "Bone up on your appetite."

I met famous people who made the music we all grew up with Carl Perkins, Ringo Starr, BB King, Johnny Cash, Loretta Lynn, and Carla Thomas. The Marks to The Bar Keys, Steve Croper to Al Gore, became friends with George Kline and Rufus Thomas. Randy Trywick came by the station wanting me to listen to his new record. Later, he became Randy Travis.

George Strait opened for my Elvis character at a live concert.

Red West, an old friend of Elvis, broke down and cried about a book he and some guys in the old Memphis mafia wrote. Spent a summer doing Visit Tennessee TV AD for the state tourism department with Dolly Parton. Almost went to jail with Jerry Jeff Walker, which became the "Battle of the Waffle House." I stole Tom T. Hall's limo by mistake. Got a free weekend at the Hall of Fame hotel because the manager thought I was Earl Thomas Conley. I played golf with the Blues Brothers Band. Charlie Daniels wanted to meet me because he loved my political soapboxes.

    I know I sound like a namedropper and I am bragging. Well, like I said, I grew up in a small town. To do and see what I did, still amazes me to this day. I not only saw these folks, but we were all in the same bizz. We were working together. I became a part of all that. Now let me say that after rubbing elbows with the stars, I am still in awe of the police, the firefighters, and women doctors and nurses, hospice workers, and emergency folks. Because if we all had a choice in life to choose between what is more important, a singer or law enforcement, a band or a doctor. If given the choice of The Grand Ole Opry or a hospital, we would choose the latter.

Chapter Eight

Now I have some funny stories about the stars, more than I can tell in this book. Here is a good one, the day I helped Andy Kaufman find his car keys. Jerry "The King" Lawler, the great wrestler had a feud with Latka aka Andy Kaufman of *Taxi*.

The David Lettermen Show was the showcase for the big grudge match. WMC-TV was the flagship station for Mid-South Wrestling, which it broadcast all over the region. The matches went out to thirty something TV stations and were videoed in Memphis on Saturday morning. All the big stars came: Rick Flair, The Hulk, and Stone Cold. Andy had a deal, where he was busting on wrestling on the Letterman show and David surprised Andy by inviting Jerry on the show. (See The Movie, *Man In The Moon*). Jerry slaps Andy one night on the show and the feud was on.

We were living behind WMC in this two-story riverboat captain's house built in 1896. Tom Prestojokomo was an FM DJ, who lived above me. Sometimes I would wander over there and watch the live taping. When the feud was at its height, I tried to get Andy on the morning show, but he would go into his Latka Gravas character and acted as if he did not understand. He did that to me about three or four times.

Well one day, I saw Andy searching his car, so I walked over to the parking lot and he hollered at me for help. I walked over and he is almost crying because he could not find his car keys. He was talking a mile a minute about how he had them in his pocket and blah blah blah. Finally, he says, "Can you please help me?" Well in my best imitation of his Taxi TV Character Latka, I said, "San on nan mookat ola." The look on his face was priceless. He was wearing a neck brace because Jerry "The King" had hurt his neck on the Lettermen show. Well, he slung that brace off and threw it at the car. I thought he was going to hit me and he turns away from me and lo and behold, I saw his keys in the ignition and said, "Have you tried looking in your ignition switch?" He looks and sees them, opens the door, gets in, backs out, and looks at me and say "Thank you much."

When I started on the radio in Columbia, I was on the air from a.m. until 10 a.m. and usually stayed at the station until 1 p.m. doing promo work, doing the editing myself. By the time I got to Memphis, I was off at 10 a.m. to play golf and back home to do a little writing for the next day's show. Life was good.

Trips to Nashville for the Country Music Seminar from my time in Memphis and Winston-Salem included encounters with many famous country singers and songwriters. I always like songwriters better. They seemed to have more passion. One of those was Harlan Howard, who wrote songs for Patsy Cline such as "I Fall To Pieces." I encountered Harlan in the Long Horn Steak House in Nashville, where they served a drink named for him that included vodka and cranberry juice as his doctors warned him that drinking was going to kill him, but if he had to drink, drink cranberry juice, as it was good to clean out his system. I asked him once why he did not write a book about his experiences in country music. He told he wrote his book in his songs.

I ran into a few NFL Quarterbacks over the years. I found myself sitting with Troy Aikman of the Dallas Cowboys as we both waited on the doors to open for a luncheon in Nashville. A favorite was Terry Bradshaw, who won four Super Bowls with the Pittsburgh Steelers. Tammy and I were out eating and noticed Bradshaw in a booth sort of out of sight. Well, Tammy walks over to talk to him and twenty minutes later calls me to come on over. He was very nice and we later saw him again on the Cayman Islands. When I yelled to him he replied, "How You Doing Clemson?"

Vince Gill was playing in the Crosby Golf Tournament outside Winston-Salem and came into the studio. I told him his single was number eight on the charts and would be number one next week. He was a laid back guy, who played in Pure Prairie League with Timothy Schmidt of The Eagles.

I first met Linda Ronstadt at Myrtle Beach. She was playing at a club owned by Howard Beach. Three guys in her backup band later became The Eagles, Don Henley, Glenn Frye, and Bernie Leadon. I was mesmerized by Linda. She was beautiful and could cuss like a sailor. Of all the bands I have heard, The Eagles reproduced their studio sound on stage. No lip-syncing there. I once went to a concert with two beautiful women only to have The Eagles invite them back stage and I never saw them again.

Walter Payton of the Chicago Bears came into the studio promoting a children's book he wrote. He was one of the nicest people and I see why they called him "Sweetness." I was once kicked out of a Ted Nugent party. Country legend Loretta Lynn was a person true to h beliefs. With her, you got what you saw and if you did not like it, too bad. Vanna White of the TV Show *Wheel of Fortune* and I had a connection as we both hailed from South Carolina, she from Myrtle

Beach and me from Columbia. When Bill Dotson and I did Aunt Eloise, Red Foxx of *Sanford and Son* came on. We got him to do promos saying, "Eat more possum."

One night in Memphis Les Acree, Bill Dotson and I were supposed to meet Tom T. Hall and his limousine. Well, an ice storm hit, Tom T. did not make it, but his car and driver did. While we waited the record promoter said, "Let's steal it." We "borrowed" Tom T. Hall's limousine. We went pub-crawling all over town in a 1957 black Cadillac that had enough metal in it to build four Toyotas with a Tom T. license plate. Push a button, a liquor cabinet opened up. Push another button a television opened up. We went to T-Tommy's Steak House, the Rendezvous, and Blues Alley off Beale Street and made it back about 4 a.m. still without Tom T. Hall. The bill went to the record company.

There was once talk of Aunt Eloise, the television show. In the early days of cable, many saw the future of channels for different things such as a golf channel. I am still waiting for that phone call. There was a show in Memphis called Almost Alive, like a poor man's Saturday Night Live. I did a character on there called Hosea Cosellis, an Hispanic Howard Cosell.

I once did a character in Memphis called Clara Voyant, an Astrologer who read horoscopes. Well, one listener threatened a lawsuit saying I stole his character. Les Acree assembled Howard Scripp lawyers for the meeting and we scared the guy to death. The lawyers took me out for steak and lobster at the Bombay Bicycle Club, as they loved coming to Memphis especially if the work was that easy.

Once in Memphis, there was talk of big snowstorm. Bill Dotson and I decided to stay at a hotel a few block from the station, so we could be on the air the next morning. I spent the night relaxing in a hot tub. The next morning I grabbed a newspaper from the lobby and looked out the front door to see twenty-seven inches of snow on the ground. We walked three blocks through snow up to our waists.

Aunt Eloise almost went to the great beyond in a balloon once in Memphis. Kellogg cereal had a balloon and I found myself in it high above the Mississippi River one day doing on air radio, but then the wind picked up. The pilot took us down, we hit three times, bounced, and I jumped out of the balloon, but it continued on landing in some trees and a swamp. The truck following got stuck in the mud.

Well, the day and the near tragedy was not over. A helicopter picked me up, but it had engine failure on the way back and did an emergency landing on a spit of land right off the bank of Mud Island. It was amazing how the pilot landed it going counter clockwise. I almost died twice in one day. This would happen to me again when I got sick at WTQR.

Another helicopter story in Memphis involved Captain Pat Adams of the Memphis Police, who did traffic for us on the radio. He once gave Elvis a ticket and then got a call to do security for him and became friends with "The King." Adams once did security when Elvis rented out the Liberty Land Amusement Park. This was when Elvis was dating Natalie Wood.

Another adventure in Memphis was the Battle of Waffle House. Bob Tucker of the Bill Black Combo once opened for The Beatles at the Hollywood Bowl. He said of The Beatles that he could not understand a word they said due to their thick English accents. The Bill Black Combo included Jimmy Neil, Johnny Burton, and Mike Utley on keyboards. They were my back up band when I did Bo Bo Boatwright, the world's worst Elvis Impersonator. Bob Tucker taught music at Memphis State University, when not playing music.

Bob and I were going down to hear Kris Kristofferson and Rita Coolidge at Kenney Roger's Hideaway, not the Kenny Rogers who sang with Dolly Parton. I ran into Kristofferson accidentally. Not a very big man like myself, he politely said, "Excuse me." He wrote some great songs such as "Me and Bobby McGee," "For the Good Times," "Sunday Morning' Coming Down," and "Help Me Make It Through the Night."

Larry Rogers, who was in the Bill Black Combo after Black died in 1965 produced Alan Jackson, Garth Brooks, and Rick Nelson's last album, which has never been released due to litigation among his heirs.

Jerry Jeff Walker joined the threesome, which really made the group seventeen as Jerry Jeff had fourteen personalities. Walker wrote songs such as "Up Against the Wall, Redneck Mother, and LA Freeway and Mr. Bojangles."

On this night with Jerry Jeff Walker, I got talking about Jimmy Buffet. Walker said he took Buffet to Key West to Louie's Backyard, the club where an MCA Records Representative signed Buffet.

Back in Memphis this night, we went looking for somewhere to jam and the adult beverages flowed liberally. Jerry was driving a rental car and somewhere around Mount Mariah, we got lost and got the car stuck in the median, and called a tow truck. We walked to a nearby Waffle House, where the previously hungry Jerry Jeff went numb saying "I ain't hungry" and fell asleep. Ralph Jordan, who was a DJ at WLVS, owned by Sam Phillips, who discovered Elvis, walked over. He had tried to reveal Aunt Eloise's identity as previously stated during an Alabama concert in Memphis. For his trouble, Jerry Jeff cussed Jordan, who aroused from his stupor.

About this time, if it could not get any stranger, the Memphis Police walk in looking for the owner of the car stuck in the median. Well, I knew Captain Pat of the Memphis Police. He did traffic for the morning show. We contacted him and escaped going to jail. We waited until the tow truck came and that ended the Battle of the Waffle House.

SHANIA TWAIN

Chapter Nine

T-Tommy's Western Steak House and Lounge was a favorite hang out of mine in Memphis. You entered the place and got a metal plate. You chose your cut of meat and it was cooked on the plate. They gave it back to you on a wooden platter and warned you the plate was very hot.

Everybody in Memphis went to T-Tommy's Western Steak House and Lounge. *Walking Tall,* remember that movie? The real Buford Pusser use to eat there and he looked a lot like Joe Don Baker, the actor who played him in the movie. The Rock did a version of that movie as well. Buford was not very talkative and he had the battle scars to prove he had dealt with some tough folks, but I liked him.

Tammy Wynette came in to T-Tommy's with Tom Collins. You dedicated country fans may remember a song Merle Haggard wrote for Tommy. He and Tammy were dating at this time and she was low key, but very nice to me.

Jock Mahoney was a big western star and even played Tarzan in a couple of flicks. He had many funny stories to tell about John Wayne and some of his leading ladies. He never busted on anybody. He seemed to be content, retired, and going around the world in the old west movie star's tour. They came once a year and all the western stars came to T-Tommy's. He knew everybody.

Pat Bertram of *Green Acres* fame played in many westerns with Hop Along Cassidy and Roy Rogers. Bertram, who played Mr. Haney on *Green Acres*, told this funny story. He said when Trigger, Roy's horse died, he had him stuffed. When Bullet, the dog died, Roy had him stuffed. Dale Evans, Roy's wife always slept with one eye open until the day Roy Rogers died, as she was afraid she would have the same fate.

T–Tommy's became my hangout in the early 1980s in Memphis. I only lived a few blocks away at the time. T had a pinball machine, old time pay off called Sun Valley. You had to shake and jerk to get those balls in the right hole. I could take a roll of quarters and play all night.

The Mayor of Memphis and many city officials hung out there well. Singer songwriter John Prine would drop by along with Charlie Rich and Jerry Lee Lewis. T-Tommy's had a booth way up in back of the club and you could see everything from front door, lower room dining hall, and the stage, but nobody could see you. The back entrance led straight to that booth and T-Tommy called it the Elvis booth.

T- Tommy helped Elvis out in his early years to few steaks. Everybody knows that Elvis could not go anywhere without a bunch of fans mobbing him, so he asked T if he could come down and get a steak. Well, Elvis would sneak up the back way with a cowboy hat or fake beard, sit in that back table and eat. One night T-Tommy was having A Elvis Presley Singing Contest with $100 dollar first prize. Elvis called Tommy and said he would like to enter the contest. Tommy said, "No way Elvis, they know who you are. No Elvis, Colonel Parker would sue me." Elvis said, "T you get that booth ready I will be there." T- Tommy was as nervous as an expectant father.

The club held about 200 people max. A lounge down stairs in the back with my Sun Valley pin ball machine, a few chairs and couch with RCA Color TV along with two floor sets, with a bar and twenty stools. The upstairs had a stage for the band and another twenty tables and five booths in the back. Elvis's booth was in the corner.

That night Tommy tells himself Elvis is not coming. Well as soon as the contest started, there were at least six Elvis impersonators walking around the club dressed in their finest Elvis suit. This was 1970s, so the Las Vegas Elvis in cape and rhinestones was in vogue.

Well, here comes the real Elvis. He sits in that booth. At first T was not sure who it was because this person in the Elvis booth was sporting a full beard and an aviator cap, like the World War II pilots wore. Tommy goes over to table to tell this person the table is reserved and sees it is Elvis. "Elvis are you crazy?" He smiles and says introduce me as "Aaron from Tupelo." Aaron was Elvis's middle name. T shakes h[is] hand. "Elvis we got six guys. You want me to call you last."Elvis says, "Call me up third."

So friends I am here to tell you history was made. The contestant number one dressed out in the white jump suit just like Elvi[s] wore on tour that summer. The folks gave him a ten. Next, one dressed all in black leather like Elvis's 1968 TV show. He gets a 10. T-Tommy brings on Aaron or the real Elvis with beard, khaki pants, and shirt, wearing a WW2 Aviator cap. He sings and the audience gives him a six. The next three all decked out in different Elvis jump suits get a 10, 10, and 9. When it is all said and done, Elvis finished off a t-bone steak, left the server, a 100-dollar tip, and came in third.

Now you are saying, "How did he get third place with three gu[ys] ahead of them?" Well, two of the Elvises got in fight, T-Tommy threw them out, and the other Elvis impersonator had to leave because four eyewitnesses said his wife showed up and did not like the women he was with. Elvis wound up third in his own contest.

T-Tommy told me that Elvis could never eat another steak the[re] because the Memphis newspaper printed the story the next day about Elvis coming in third in his own contest. We can only think what Colonel Parker said after that because as far as I know, that is the only free concert Elvis did, even if it was one song.

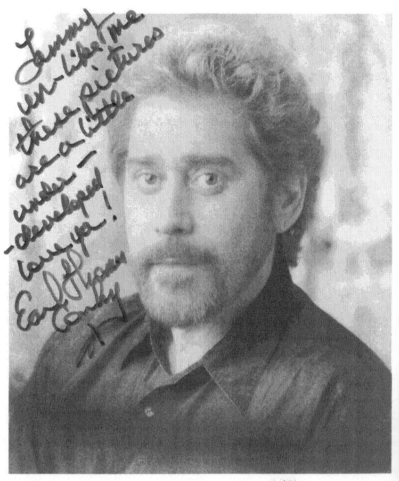

EARL THOMAS CONLEY

Booking:
Buddy Lee Attraction
38 Music Square East
(615) 244-4336

Chapter Ten

Memphis sits on the Mississippi River just across from Arkansas. I always thought people in Nashville thought Memphis was in Arkansas. One year on July 4th, Dan Lancaster, who owned a postcard business in Memphis and a docked riverboat. He invited Aunt Eloise up to the Pilot House. It was at night and there were 300,000 people along the river with barges loaded with fireworks ready to go off with synchronized music. There were speakers three miles up and down the river and Dan invited me to speak to the people. "Good Evening! Good Evening! Good Evening!" went up and down the Mississippi River before the fireworks lit up the sky that year.

Well, back to food, a recurring theme in this book. In Memphis, Huey's was near the radio station, not to mention the drug store on Union Avenue, which had the best double cheeseburger all greasy in wax paper I ever had.

There are great stories in Memphis such as the time I went to Jerry Lee Lewis's 50th birthday party at Kenney Roger's Hideaway. Well, 8 p.m. and no Jerry Lee and I have to be on the radio at 6 a. m. Well, 11 p.m. and no Jerry Lee. Jerry Lee still not there at 1 a.m. and I am thinking I have waited this long and I am going to see "The Killer." Jerry

Lee shows about 3 a.m. feeling no pain. He got wild, tearing up a baby grand piano, he always had to have a baby grand.

I saw Jerry Lee at a Christmas Show once with Joe South, who wrote some great songs such as "Hush," "Games People Play," "Rose Garden," and "Don't It Make You Wanna Go Home." Among those at the party was Ron Wood of *The Rolling Stones*. I never understood a word he said due to his thick British accent, but I partied with a Rolling Stone.

I worked with Bill Dotson in Memphis. Many do not realize that we broadcasted United States Football League (USFL) for the Memphis Showboats. It was great as the league played games from March through May and their home field was the Liberty Bowl, where I saw Alabama's Paul "Bear" Bryant coach his last college game.

The coach of the Showboats was Pepper Rogers, who was not lively personality, but he had some players that sure were. Among the was Reggie White, who later played in the NFL for the Philadelphia Eagles and won a Super Bowl with the Green Bay Packers. Reggie was the funniest human being I ever encountered. He did an Elvis impersonation up and down the aisle of the airplane while traveling along with some very politically incorrect things that will not make the pages of this book.

Life on the radio with the Showboats started on Friday with lunch on the airplane for Sunday games, followed by a bus ride to the hotel, a bus ride to the field for a workout, a bus ride to eat dinner and then a bus ride back to the hotel. Saturday it was back on the bus to the field and then back to the hotel for evening free time before the Sunday games.

Man, those guys sure did eat well. I had my first encounter with chicken cordon bleu and steaks, but the press box cuisine was hit or miss. Hit was the time former quarterback Johnny Unitas served us Maryland Fried Chicken at Byrd Stadium when the Showboats played the Baltimore Stars saying, "Ya'll will love it." Unitas had played for the Baltimore Colts before they moved to Indianapolis.

There was the time the Showboats played the Houston Gamblers at the Astrodome. A football comes flying by I tried to catch it, but missed. I picked it up, threw it back, and realized I just missed catching a pass from Jim Kelly, who later led the Buffalo Bills to four straight Super Bowls. The food in Texas was awesome. There were two whole sides of beef rotating on a spit and when they served it, this guy pulls out a scimitar or a giant Bowie knife to slice it onto the plates.

Now the bad side to the press box food was the Los Angeles Coliseum, where an Olympics was once held and the Southern Californ Trojans play. It was like an Alamo of a press box with little tiny holes to look out and we got a box lunch. The stadium was in Little Havana in Universal City and who do I encounter, but my old Memphis nemesis Rick Dees, who was signing autographed photos of himself.

I knew I was getting to Dees when he started changing the joke sheet that all radio DJs get called The Electric Weenie from a guy, Tom Adams, in Hawaii to include jokes about Aunt Eloise. "What is that gree stuff in the refrigerator? Aunt Eloise." Dees left to go to Hollywood, failed and came back to Memphis. We beat him locally in the morning slot.

Back in Memphis, my parents visited once. Les Acree and I too them down on Beale Street. A limousine pulls up beside us, the door opens and out steps Muhammad Ali, who was showing the symptoms Parkinson disease even then. It was a time of no cell phones or camera to hassle the stars. My father just looks at him and says, "That is Cassi Clay," the name Ali had before converting to Islam.

We were on our way to the Budweiser Theater to meet Carl Perkins, who wrote "Blue Suede Shoes," but my father again knew him as the man who played with Johnny Cash and for my father it was all about…Cash. Carl was on his way to do The Ed Sullivan Show when he was in a car wreck. He watched Elvis sing his song while in the hospital, but he was not bitter about it. That song sold millions of records and Carl wrote it. The royalty checks rolled in for years.

A funny story about Conway Twitty. Program Director Les Acree was leery about playing Conway's song "I Would Love To Lay You Down" due to the suggestive lyrics. Before I interviewed Conway, Les told me not to mention the song. Well, then we did not play records, but small one song tapes. Conway comes in and we start talking. I did not bring up the new single, but Conway did and the next thing I know the tape comes flying into the studio after Conway complained about Les not wanting to play it. I caught the tape and said, "Well, look a here Conway, it just flew into the studio."

As a kid, I was into Soul Music, not Heavy Metal. I liked to listen to Solomon Burke, Arthur Connelly, Otis Redding and Al Green. I went to Al Green's church in Memphis. He preached and sang some inspirational

Gospel songs. I had paid to see him in concert, but after that visit, I wanted to pay on the way out of the church.

There was a public golf course in Memphis. Les Acree took me there one day and introduced me to The Memphis Horns, who were in the Blue Brother's movie. I met The Barclays and told me that white guys playing with Black guys would have gotten beat up in my hometown. They laughed. I spent many Mondays and Thursdays playing golf at the course with these guys.

In Memphis, I got to know Rufus Thomas, a DJ on WDIA, the first Black radio station in town. He was the father of Carla Thomas, who sang the "Funky Chicken." Black and White relations were not good in Memphis. Being known as the place Martin Luther King, Jr. lost his life was a handicap. Rufus took me to the Lorraine Motel to the room King stayed in and nearby to the boarding house from where James Earl Ray shot King. I stood in that window myself and it was unnerving. There was a campaign about that time to bring Memphis together. I remember what Rufus said to me about the piano. "It takes both Black and White keys to play the Star Spangled Banner."

Another story involving Rufus. We were doing commercials together at ARK Studios near the radio station. I was renting a room from Tom Jackamo in a Riverboat Captain's House. One day, I was standing out on the porch when I saw a bus pull up. The driver told me he was trying to find ARK Studios. Well, I jumped on the bus to show him and came face to face with ZZ Top, who were there to record their TV Dinners album. I never liked that record much because I heard it a million times while they recorded in an adjoining studio.

Rufus Thomas was on WDIA in Memphis. He had a white Mercedes that he put a sunroof in once. He was a walking history book on music. When he started DJing, many sponsors left, but came back when they realized Black people buy stuff too.

Here is a story Rufus told me. Otis Redding started as a roadie for Stax Records. One day Otis asked to do a song. Steve Cropper said sure and they recorded "These Arms of Mine." The rest is history.

PAM TILLIS
www.pamtillis.com

Chapter Eleven

I remember when Elvis died. Jimmy Griffith owned Castaways in Myrtle Beach. He always had a Burger King cooler full of Purple Jesus or Tequila Sunrise. He told me that Elvis had died in Memphis. Tears were rolling down both of our faces. People today might not realize that "The King" was just as popular with men and women. The next day, I went out and bought every newspaper I could find even though they all had the same stories. Little did I know that one day I would do the first radio broadcast from Graceland.

Once while still in Columbia I had an Elvis Film Festival. Dewey Corbin owned the Starlight Drive-In. I dated his daughter and operated the projector. We came up with the idea of holding an Elvis movie festival one night. We showed four movies and I cleared $3,000.

During my time in Memphis, I did a character called Bo Bo Boatwright, the World's Worst Elvis Impersonator. I only did "That's Alright Momma" at fairs and such. It was so quick and funny that nobody was left wanting more. One night George Strait opened for Bo Bo.

I met many people with connections to Elvis. Bobby Neil, Jr. once showed me a video tape he had of Elvis playing in the swimming pool with Bobby as a kid. His father was Elvis's first manager. I asked him why he did not sell it and he told me it was something personal and he did not need the money. One can just imagine how much home movies of Elvis in the early days would be worth.

I encountered the man who gave Elvis his start, Sam Phillips of Sun Studios. Today, the building that tourist know as the studio was actually a garage. They moved all the equipment into the present day site, but it is not the same building. When Johnny Cash, Waylon Jennings, Willie Nelson and Kris Kristofferson recorded the Highwayman album, we were invited to the Peabody Hotel Ball Room for a kickoff party. After hours, we all went to Sun Studios, where I met Sam Phillips. He told stories about he was looking for a White man to sound like a Black man and he found one in Elvis Presley. In 1957, he sold Elvis to RCA Records for $35,000, the equivalent of $100,000 today, but he was not bitter. It was enough money for him to live and he never went hungry.

Doing the first radio broadcast from inside Graceland gave me an interesting viewpoint. I found Priscilla Presley to be very prepared, very professional and VERY beautiful. I met Uncle Vester, Elvis's uncle, who worked security. He was a character and told me about Elvis's monkey, Scatter, who liked to throw feces on people who got too close to his cage. I was doing a radio break on WMC 79 and did not realize there was a tour group behind me. When I finished and turned around, I got a standing ovation. Well, they were standing and applauding.

People asked me if I met Elvis, but he was dead before I got to Memphis, but that never stopped me from saying I met "The King." I would say, "Oh Yeah, I met him. He loved me on the radio. Elvis hated Rick Dees, but he loved me. Elvis was a good boy. He was good to his Momma. I went swimming with him at Graceland." Once I got them hooked. I told them he gave me a shirt from one of his movies. They said, "Wow!" Then I would start to get emotional, choking back tears as I told them that once Elvis asked me for a Pepsi while we were hanging by the pool. I went and got him one. When I returned, (fake tears now really starting to flow), he looked up at me. They asked, "Yes, what did he say?" I said Elvis looked at me and said, "Thank you. Thank you very much." I would burst out laughing and they knew they had been had.

I do remember once when Elvis came to town and I approached Wayne Edwards of RCA about getting some tickets comped. He laughed and told me NO ONE got free tickets to Elvis. Elvis had to pay for his mother, father, girlfriends, etc. to attend a concert.

Tammy loved to take people on tours of Memphis, the eight years we lived there. Tammy worked for W. B. Tanner and Co. They recorded radio jingles, would trade out advertising to do jingles for the station, and made their money from the customers. We met many famous people while there. We wrangled an invitation to Danny Thomas's St. Jude soiree at the Colonial Country Club and the W. B. Tanner home as well. We were greeted at the door by a robot and got cigar from Mr. Tanner. Danny Thomas gave us a history lesson for ten or fifteen minutes and we met his daughter Marlo, "That Girl," and her husband, Phil Donahue.

Earlier in the day at the Pro-Am golf tournament that raised money, I encountered Phil along with Bob Hope, who was old, but still could bring the one liners. While Phil was playing, I yelled at him once saying, "Hey, Phil I got all your records." Truth is I enjoyed his television show and recorded it on VHS every day. Some great material for radio on that show.

Another person I met then was Forrest Tucker, who was famous for the TV show *FTroop*, but I knew him for movies like the *Sands of Iwo Jima*, which he starred in with John Wayne. I learned that many of the actors were stereotyped due to their television shows, but when you brought up their movie careers, you got a very different reaction. They appreciated being remembered for what I think they considered serious acting.

Another person like that was Ernest Borgnine, who won an Oscar for *Marty*. Most people then knew him for the television show *McHale's Navy*. I knew he was in town in Memphis once and called the hotel, got through to him, and got him on the radio station. I did it by talking about his movie career. He was in some good Spencer Tracy films.

While in Memphis, I met George Cline, who was Elvis's best man, and other members of the "Memphis Mafia" such as Red West. George never wrote about Elvis. Frank Leveler worked security for Elvis and got "The King" some women to come back stage after concerts. Frank became the President of American Polygram Records and later managed James Brown.

My aunt married James Brown, the Godfather of Soul. Marie Black was the Justice of the Peace in Barnwell, South Carolina. One day James Brown came in wanting to get married and she performed the ceremony. Two weeks later James was back wanting to get a divorce assuming that since Marie married him, she could give a divorce too.

James was not my uncle, but one could only imagine Aunt Eloise and Uncles James Brown on the radio together.

Once James was arrested for shooting his car when it broke down. They took him to jail. One night in Nashville, a group of DJs and I were enjoying some liquid encouragement via the Jack Daniels Distiller Bar in the Opryland Hotel. We began chanting "Free James Brown! Free James Brown!" The next day the USA Today had a story in it "Country DJs Hold Rally To Free James Brown."

I saw James in concert and he had this great thing he did at the end of the shows. He acted exhausted, his people placed a cape around him, and began to lead him off the stage. At this moment someone would say, "Ladies and Gentleman, James Brown, the hardest working man in show business." At this point, Brown would throw off the cape and return to the microphone to continue the concert. This happened several times before the show finally ended.

Aunt Eloise had her only big hit while in Memphis. "Light, Gas, and Robbery" was parodied from a hit by the Oak Ridge Boys bemoaning a rate hike by Memphis Light, Gas and Water. Produced by Larry Rodger and recorded at Lyn Lou Studios, it came in the Sunday newspaper. The flip side was by T. G. Sheppard.

This might be a good place to discuss Aunt Eloise and possum. While in Memphis the Great Possum Chilly Fest occurred attended by 20 to 30 thousand people and sponsored by the Memphis Press Centaur newspaper. It began with a "Genuine" chilly possum recipe.

Once at the Blues Award Convention in Memphis I met B. B. King and got to sit on stage with him. I had a good time in Memphis and I am amazed kids from Eastover, South Carolina, ever got to see the things I did or meet the people I did.

Tammy and I had our first daughter while in Memphis. Tara Dennis Young joined our family in 1983.

LINDA DAVIS

CREDIT: JIM McGUIRE 9/90A

Chapter Twelve

Radio was good to me through the years. I loved my job and the freedom to speak out and make people laugh. It was never about the money. It was what I loved and I was blessed to have a job I enjoyed going to everyday.

Before I left Memphis to go to WTQR in Winston-Salem, North Carolina, I was offered more money to stay, but instead of a thirteen-hour road trip or ninety-minute plane trip, it was a three-hour ride home and a three-hour trip to Clemson if I moved to Winston-Salem. I missed seeing my folks and only got to go home a few times a year. Moving to Winston-Salem was a cut in pay, but I could go home on the weekend and after eight years go see my Clemson Tigers play football.

Clemson Tiger football has always been a favorite past time for me. Ever since I was a kid picking cotton in the field for my Country Grandfather, I was drawn to the agricultural university in the state of South Carolina. Watching the Frank Howard Show on television was a part of life in my home. My Uncle Tom was a member of IPTAY (I Pay Ten A Year) supporting Clemson athletic scholarships. My Aunt ToToo, Tom's sister, was a big Clemson fan. Other members of my family attended the school in northwest South Carolina and I would have tried too, but they did not have a broadcast school. Therefore, my dreams of radio ended up in Columbia at the University of South Carolina, but I still think that tiger paw symbol is the coolest thing that ever was invented.

When Clemson played Nebraska for the National Championship in college football in the Orange Bowl in Miami, Florida, I was there. Although our camper did break down at the Georgia/Florida state line, we made it to the game. What a scene we found there with police on horseback and Hare Krishna chanting on the streets. We parked and a Cuban kid offered to protect our vehicle for $5. I paid and when we returned the Cornhusker vehicles around us were trashed, but the kid was there and our vehicle was safe.

I came to WTQR through the man who discovered me in Columbia at WCOS and took me to Memphis, Les Acree. I started with Billy Buck Blevins, who was the king of morning radio in Winston-Salem and we hit it off pretty good. Billy was an easygoing fellow, but I knew he wanted to move up to the management level. He would have made great program director too.

My whole life I had used humor to smooth things over with folks that I had problems. Billy was no different and we had a lot of fun. The first few weeks we were getting to know each other on and off the air.

Buck and I were just good old southern boys living our dreams. I made Buck laugh and as time went by, we got to where we liked each other a lot. Anybody that knew Buck thought the world of him, but he has always been his man on the air, so I had to try hard to make him like me and we did reach a friendship that remains today. Buck had genuine laugh and it was not faked; it was as honest as they come.

After a couple of years with Buck, he wanted to move up. About three months before he went to the tell management he was leaving, he told me about it. I appreciated that a lot and I never said a word to the boss. Many people would have gone straight to the boss and said, "Hey Buck told me so and so," but not me. He was my friend and I never said a word. I wanted to make it radio myself and not back stab people.

Billy Buck finally said he was moving on and I understood and that left me and Les to find a replacement. For a while, I did the morning show with Les, Chuck Webster, "Mr. Bluegrass," and Danny Hall. All great people, but Les was Program Director. Chuck had his thing and so did Danny. So, off to Nashville we went for the CRS (Country Radio Seminar), where the DJs hang with stars for a week and boy do I have stories to tell about those years. The seminar was to find a new host for the show and we found him in Dale Mitchell.

Dale would have been a great movie star, tall, handsome, and could talk a volcano to stop spewing lava. He had a great laugh. In fact, it was infectious. Even if you thought a joke was not funny his laugh would make you laugh. Just a good old boy from Catties, Kentucky, as he would describe himself.

He was our midday guy in Memphis and did the weekend weather for WMC-TV. He was great on TV. I always wondered why he did not stick with TV because I thought he had a great future on television. The good morning show stayed in the number one slot with Dale for the next few years in Winston-Salem.

Les Acree, who was my program director at WMC and WTQR, landed his dream job at WIVK Knoxville. Les was a big Tennessee Volunteer fan, WIVK was the flagship radio station for Tennessee Football, and he was closer to home. I hated to see Les go, but glad for him because I understood his reason. I would say my dream job would have been to land a job at the flagship station for Clemson, which includes tickets, free press parking, and the press box food is great.

I went to many Tennessee football games with Les Acree. After each game, we brought the tape back to Memphis arriving at 2 a.m.

with the game to be broadcast that morning at 11 a.m. There were no satellites then, so we brought the tape back for many weeks. Over the years, I think I went to 26 Tennessee games and only two games at Clemson.

I once encountered Lewis Grizzard at a CMA meeting, where he was a keynote speaker. He wrote for the Atlanta newspaper and books such as *Elvis Is Dead And I Am Not Feeling Too Good Myself*. I was standing at Rachel's Restaurant waiting on Les Acree. Lewis was reading a newspaper. He asked me about the food. I told him it was good, but they could not stand Georgia fans, only Clemson fans. Lewis grinned real big and he joined Les and myself for some food. Lewis was a big Georgia Bulldog fan and he had heart problems. He had a pig valve in his heart.

Hank Williams, Jr. came to town with an opening act that Dale had met at a showcase show in Nashville. A showcase is where the record labels bring in program directors from around the country to listen to the new talent they are developing. Dale asked me to go to the show that I had to see a guy who was great. At this time in radio, I stopped going to most concerts. To be honest, I was just jaded somewhat and being back stage at shows was not a big deal to me after twenty some years of Friday and Saturday concerts I was enjoying staying home and grilling out. I have been getting up at 4 a.m. and going to bed by 9 p.m. for so long. I loved staying home and sitting up until midnight.

Well, I went with Dale that night and after slapping hands with Hank and his crew, we went over to meet this new soon to be star. Now I have seen thousands of acts before and one out of ten actually makes the big time. We walked into his dressing room there sat a husky guy with blue jeans and white cowboy shirt and black hat. Dale gave him a big hug. In Nashville, a lot of hugging goes on between record guys, DJs and singers. It is a Nashville thing. Dale introduced me. Yep we hugged too.

He said he was an Oklahoma boy and loved the rodeo. On many of his songs, he sang about cowboys and such. He was very warm and laidback and after some small talk he was ready to open the show. Dale goes on stage, introduced himself as WTQR co-host of the morning show with me, and gets big applause. He welcomes the folks and introducing a person he calls him an up and coming star please welcome Garth Brooks. Wonder what ever happened to him?

Earl Thomas Conley (ET) and I first met at a Memphis joint called Bad Bobs. Bad Bobs during Elvis week had hosted an Elvis impersonator contest with Elvis look a likes from all over the world. They had people from Japan, Mexico, France, and Africa. Close your eyes and just think that you are in a nightclub with 100 Elvis impersonators. Short, fat, skinny, tall, black, white, everywhere you looked there was Elvis. In the game room shooting pool, playing pinball at the bar lined up in a row. Go in the restroom there five Elvises in there. "Thank you, Thank You Very Much." I was telling this story to a bunch of folks when Earl came over to see what everybody was laughing about. I told him that story and he had tears coming out his eyes laughing so hard. We became friends and many times when I was in Nashville, we would hook up go to eat and check out some clubs.

He had a show coming up in Greensboro I invited him and Frank Level, a former big dog at Mercury Records to stay at my house for the weekend. I found out ET was on the patch. The patch was just that round nicotine patch that you wore to help quit smoking.

ET must have had ten packs of Juicy Fruit chewing gum in his pocket to help him quit. He chewed 24 hours a day, I do believe. Well on the radio Friday morning, I asked our listeners to help me pull a joke on ET. I told them that he was trying to quit smoking and how much he chewed Juicy Fruit gum. I asked the folks that were coming to the show to buy a couple packs Juicy Fruit and when ET is introduced and came on stage to lob a few packs up on the stage. Well ET walks out, the band cranks up, and here come a few hundred packs of Juicy Fruit gum flying at him. So many packs were thrown on stage they had to get a push broom to clear off. I was standing off stage and Earl Thomas looks back at me and in the mike says "Eloise, I'm gonna get you." The crowd loved it and ET went on to do a great show.

Returning to my favorite theme...FOOD. There is Cooter Stew. love Cooter Stew and have been eating it since I was knee high to a Cooter. Everybody hates a nasty Cooter. You want a clean Cooter. I sometimes use a jar of vinegar and wire brush to clean the Cooter. Eating a nasty Cooter will make you sick. A Cooter will stink if you do n keep it clean. A General Manager told me once he had to pull off the side of the road laughing so hard he could not drive. Now, people think when I am talking about a Cooter it is something dirty. It is a turtle that swam in ponds in South Carolina where I grew up.

Chapter Thirteen

I took my father to North Wilkesboro to the NASCAR race when there was still one there. I met Flossie Johnson, who was then married to racing legend Junior Johnson. Flossie approached me saying, "I listen to you every morning." To this day, Flossie and I remain friends. She invited me to use her cabin in the Blue Ridge Mountains and I visit her often. During this visit, my father, met one of his heroes, Enos Slaughter, who played baseball for the New York Yankees.

There was a time when NASCAR did not market the Charlotte race in Piedmont North Carolina, but that changed when Ralph Seagraves got the idea to promote the race on WTQR. Ralph was a character and it was a different time. He wore vests and odd looking belt buckles. He carried a roll of $4,000 around in his pocket and drove a gold Rolls Royce. Once on the Ralph Emery Show on CMT, it fell out of his pocket into the couch, where a later guest found it and it was returned to Seagraves.

Going to a race with Ralph was an experience. Sitting up in the skyboxes and suites was the same as sitting down in the stands. After about the first thirty laps, Ralph would say, "They are just riding around" and you would go around visiting for the next hour and a half until the race was almost over and the fun began.

Tom Chambers of Goody's headache powers, T. Wayne Robertson, and Ralph Seagraves approached WTQR about coming down to do live promos from the racetrack. Dale Mitchell and I went for six straight years. The first ticket sales went up thirty percent due to these efforts. R. J. Reynolds Tobacco sponsored NASCAR then and the driver raced for the Winston Cup. Ralph and his people carried white and red paint themselves and painted the walls white with the red Winston words around the tracks.

T. Wayne Robertson took over for Ralph Seagraves as R. J. Reynolds's man for NASCAR. He started the truck series. I remember once he told me more trucks were sold in American than cars. He had some vision. He invited Daddy and me to Rockingham once to sit in the suite. Daddy met Cale Yarborough. He once told me a story that Cale was caught for speeding and taken before the Magistrate, who let him go when he realized who he was. Robertson was killed while fishing o the Mississippi River. I remember the many funerals I attended over th years such as Denny Millsap at WTQR and my Uncle Tom's. Once at a Clemson game, we were sitting so we could see the Blue Ridge

Mountains and Lake Hartwell. Uncle Tom said he thought it was a close to heaven, as he would ever get.

Dale Mitchell and I went to Charlotte the first time and found ourselves up in the Speedway Club. WSOC was on one side and we approached the drivers after they finished with them and they all naturally just came over and let us interview them.

Over time, NASCAR changed. R. J. Reynolds got out due to the tobacco payout. Instead of being invited to participate in Charlotte, they wanted the radio station to pay to set up.

NASCAR is so different now. It is too vanilla and too many cookie cutter drivers with no personality. It has become politically correct. It disgusts me there are no races at Rockingham or North Wilkesboro. I grew up looking forward to the Southern 500 ever year. They moved the race to California for a 94,000 seat track that now barely sells 50,000 tickets, whereas Darlington sold out 60,000 easy.

People like to make fun of racing, but I tell them to go to a race and sit in the stands, not in the suites and find out what it is to watch a race with the people. Charlotte did not want anything to do with racing until the big money started rolling in and excuse my French, but there are just too many "Damned Yankees" involved. You still see a Stars and Bars in the crowd, but racing has gotten too far away from its roots.

Now, I did the Aunt Eloise character and others on radio stations across the south while at WTQR. Listeners heard stories about Uncle Tomain on radio in Panama City, Florida, Atlanta, and back home in Columbia. Jeff Roper took over as Program Director at one of these stations and when I called in for my weekly bit, he fired me over the phone and the war began. He took over at WTQR after I left, but only lasted two years. Apparently, listeners did not like his style of dirty talk and sexual innuendo.

Program Directors who were not from the South often did not understand the market we broadcast to. Once one asked me why I was talking about The Andy Griffith Show on the eve of Mayberry Days in Mount Airy instead of *American Idol* or *Dancing With The Stars*. He did not realize the yearly festival attracted many people to the area or that The Andy Griffith Show played afternoon on WFMY just before their evening news.

Speaking of The Andy Griffith Show, here is some more name dropping from television. James Best, who played Roscoe P. Coltrane of the *Dukes of Hazard*, was a favorite, but I knew him for shows like

Gunsmoke, Wagon Train and *The Andy Griffith Show*. I asked Jim how many times he got killed on *Gunsmoke*.

Another person who was a real human being was Tim Conway, who did all those hilarious skits with Harvey Korman on the *Carol Burnett Show*, usually cracking up the latter. He also starred in lots of movies including some funny ones with Don Knotts.

We moved to Advance, North Carolina. Aunt Eloise started talking about the Christmas parade in Advance making comments about it being a great thing as it only had three floats or if we could get the mule to pull the wagon everything would go off fine. The more I made fun of it the more people got behind it. Next thing you know, Highway 801 is being blocked off and 100 people have entered the parade including kids pulled by parents, the local septic tank and of course, the mule pulling a wagon. The high school band played and even Channel 3 out of Charlotte started covering the Advance Christmas parade. I never understood exactly, but the coordinator had to go to New York to get permission to block off the highway.

While at WTQR, our family grew with a new daughter, Tabitha Louise Young.

WILLIAMS ARTISTS MANAGEMENT
816 North LaCienega Boulevard
Los Angeles, CA. 90069
(213) 657-4521

RAY STEVENS

WILLIAM MORRIS AGENCY, INC
Since 1898

Chapter Fourteen

In 1986, Billy Buck was my partner on WTQR. In 1987, Dale Mitchell came on air with Aunt Eloise and did the show for nearly six years. Dale Mitchell wanted to leave Winston-Salem for a job in Savannah, Georgia. Chuck Webster and Danny Hall substituted while we looked for a permanent replacement for Dale. Howard Neman started to interview people to bring on WTQR with Aunt Eloise. Nobody in the interviews seemed to click. Then Paul Fuller walked in silhouetted against the sun with a big grin on his face and I knew almost immediately this was the guy.

I had met Paul years earlier on an airplane going from Winston-Salem to Nashville when we stopped in Charlotte for a connecting flight. He was a big person, 6 foot 4 inches tall, and was working in WSOC in Charlotte, North Carolina. He was a big lovable Teddy Bear of a man, who loved people and beer. We clicked and we became best friends.

Paul loved to nickname people and he could tease me to get me to go off on the air. We started something we called the Breakfast Club. On early morning radio, I got up at 4:30 a.m. and was going into work at five. People would send us food for breakfast. Krispy Kreme donuts were a particular weakness that led to Aunt Eloise gaining some weight.

We had "Wild Wendy" on the air with us doing location spots a Aunt Eloise could not be seen in public. Her favorite comment was hate to think I cain't." She did a spot at Hardees where the first fiv people got free breakfast. With her long blonde hair, she liked to tell u about her amorous experiences with her husband Randy mentionir often how she liked to "Ride'em cowboy."

Well, the biscuits began to flow into the radio station. Smith Patterson got in on it introducing us to Hot Pockets. Then J. B. Brown was hired to work the morning show and we started taking turns bringing in breakfast for the "Club." Brown brought in quiche one day and the look on Paul's face was priceless. His eyes rolled into his head and said, "Meat! Meat! We Eat Meat!" This led to the Breakfast Club Charter. The rules were simple. 1. MEAT. We eat Meat. 2. Must be appetizing. 3. Good Presentation. Etc.

Then Ed Scirca wanted to join the "Club." Ed was a big person frc California and he took it to a new level, as he was a chef. Next thing yc know we are eating Egg Parmesan, Boston Butt, and lots of Mexican Food. The Breakfast Club was not just for breakfast food anymore. I discovered the CALZONE.

Restaurants started sending in chefs to talk to us about their food. I gained thirty pounds. The sales staff started complaining about all these people coming in the station. This led to catering wars. Jim Burton of Rainbow Catering started setting up a tent in the parking lot. With the chicken stew, fried fish, barbeque, the sales staff stopped complaining and began coming in early to sample the cuisine.

More food stories at WTQR. Bill France of NASCAR loved hot dogs. He asked Mark Flint to come down one day. ABC-TV executives were coming to talk about doing races on television. He was going to rent a "Banquet Room" and impress them. He had drivers such as Rusty Wallace, Richard Petty, and Dale Earnhardt in tuxedos and limousines. He took them all the Pulliams Hot Dogs. Earnhardt did not like slaw on his hot dog, just mustard and chili and Aunt Eloise never had to buy a hot dog.

A few lines about the Pettys. I have interviewed Richard and Kyle many times and we crossed paths a bunch, but here is a story about Big Paul and I. Kyle's kids raised goats and some may look at this and be offended, but not Big Paul and I. They named their goats after us. Yep and to make it even stranger Big Paul the goat, impregnated me, Aunt Eloise the Goat. Yes, the wonderful world of kids gave us fodder for many radio shows and it was fun. I laughed about this and wanted to meet the Petty kids and thank them. Not every fan of the King of NASCAR, Richard Petty, is going to get his grandkids to name goats after them.

At the breaking of the ground for Victory Junction Gang, Big Paul and I were invited to attend. Big Paul could not go, so I went on my own and did not take a jacket. It turned cold that day and Cindy Farmer who was and is a TV anchor for ABC-TV, now Fox8, and I sat together and we both were freezing. We were under a large tent with most of the media and NASCAR big wigs. I told Cindy I wanted to meet the Petty kids and thank them for naming their goats after Big Paul and me. Cindy thought that was so funny.

I saw Kyle and told him I want to meet his kids and ask them about the goats. He said to stick around they will be here. Therefore, for the next hour, we froze sitting under that tent listing to the Governor, Senator, and everybody talk about Victory Junction.

Actor Paul Newman was there to speak and I forgot about the cold weather and hung on his every word. Cindy's news crew came to get her for a live news spot and I went looking for Austin Petty and his sister to thank them for naming the goats. I finally saw them and after laughing with them about the goats, I turned and there he was, Paul Newman. I stuck my hand out, he shook it, and all that I could say was "So Butch Do You Think We Used Too Much Dynamite," a line from his movie *Butch Cassidy and the Sundance Kid.* He just smiled with those big baby blue eyes and went on shaking hands with people. I went back to my truck, forgot the cold, and said to myself, "Nobody will ever believe this."

In 1997, Big Paul and I received the CMA Award for Most Popular Radio Personality in Large Market, but Aunt Eloise could not accept the award as no one could see Aunt Eloise. Big Paul and my mother accepted the award. They were on television on CBS during the CMA show. We had one problem during the trip. The Toyota we were driving got rammed from behind and we had to tie the trunk down with shoestring. When we arrived among a sea of limousines, it must have looked like the Beverly Hillbillies had arrived. We untied the trunk, removed the luggage and then Daddy had to pay $12 to park, which did not sit too well with the military man he was inside. While Daddy grumbled, Momma was in heaven. She was going to be on TV. She got special service including a trip to the beauty parlor.

I had another mission. Ralph Seagraves, who ran marketing for R. J. Reynolds Winston Cup Series of NASCAR, had a son Colbert Seagraves, who did the same as his father for the Drag Racing Series. Colbert's wife Mary was sick with cancer and she loved the Key Lime pie that the Opryland Hotel served. My mission was to return one of these pies back to Winston-Salem, North Carolina.

Daddy did not want to attend the ceremony. He decided to watch the show from the hotel room on the television. He took a nap. Paul took charge of Momma through the rehearsal and the actual show. I found myself in the Jack Daniels Distillery Bar in the Opryland Hotel. I was telling the bartender about the award when two ladies approached me and we began to have a good time. Naïve as I was sometimes, I did not realize that they were "Ladies of the Night." So there I am doing characters for them such as Aunt Eloise, Alphonso, and Elvis. The buildup resulted in Momma and Big Paul being on CBS for exactly three seconds. I tried to call Daddy on my gigantic cell phone, but the hotel had some sort of dampening field, so I had to use the house phone. He answered the phone and said, "She was only on for three seconds."

While all this was going on, Big Paul and Momma were at the "After Party," where she met Alan Jackson, Garth Brooks, and George

Jones, with her mouth open for most of the evening. So my Momma, Frieda Young, now eighty years old still working for an Ophthalmologist in Columbia, South Carolina, for one night was Country Music Royalty.

I still had a mission. I got the Key Lime pie and personally carried it on the plane. It rode back to Greensboro on my lap and was delivered to Colbert Seagraves's wife as I had promised it would be. Aunt Eloise kept her word to a dying woman.

Chapter Fifteen

WSJS and WTQR were sister stations in Winston-Salem, so we knew all the people on 600 AM. Among these guys were Glenn Scott and Gene Overby. Gene got sick with cancer, but he had such a positive attitude about it. Once at Halloween, he showed up in a silver casket. I visited him on his sick bed. The Press Box at the Lawrence Joel Memorial Coliseum where Wake Forest plays basketball is the Gene Overby Press Room.

Before my City Granddaddy died in Columbia, I got the chance to visit him on his sick bed and thank him for the start in radio. It is good to be able to tell people who have influenced your life what they mean to you while they are still alive. I was glad to be able to spend time with my grandfather and Gene Overby.

Glenn Scott and Gene Overby did the broadcasts for Wake Forest football and basketball and I have some stories. Once during a winter storm I offered my four wheel drive Ford Blazer to get them to the Greensboro Coliseum for a UNC/Wake basketball game. At some point after we got to the game, I realized I locked my keys in the Blazer and after some climbing around I managed to get in and started out the back of the vehicle and came face to face with the bus carrying the

Tarheels and there staring at me was the bus driver and Dean Smith himself peering over the glasses on his nose, both probably wondering why this fool was climbing out of the back of a Blazer.

Early in my days at WTQR, I got a chance to go see Wake Forest play Clemson in football at Death Valley as a guest of the Gene and Glen. Once we arrived, I met Bob Bradley, a big man at Clemson. When he discovered I was a Clemson fan, he carried me all over the stadium meet people. I got to sit with my uncle at the game. It was a rough ride home as Clemson won 84-27.

I went with Glenn to the Vantage Championships, where the Senior PGA Golf Tour played at Tanglewood. I remember seeing Ross Johnson of R. J. Reynolds, who was driving around in a gold golf cart that day. He was famous for the book and movie *Barbarians at the Gate*. In the latter, he was played by Jim Garner. He moved Reynolds Atlanta, which was not a popular move.

I played with Charley Pride in the Pro-Am and when you played with Charley, you walked. You did not ride. Charlie told stories about early days in country music and what being an African-American involved. He told story about when he came out on stage and sang, "Kiss an Angel Good Morning," which was a short song and then heard silence when the audience realized he was Black. Like a scene from the movie *Blazing Saddles* a little lady would say, "You're a...You're a..." and Pride would say, "A Country Singer," which would cause everyone to laugh.

I have always thought a racist is a person who can tell what color you are on the phone, while a person who is not, does not care. I think people are too touchy today about race. Sticks and stones may break my bones, but words will never hurt me is a good way to go through life. That leads me to a character I developed as a coping mechanism for racism without being mean spirited.

Another NASCAR related story involves my character, Alphonso Willingham, NASCAR's #1 Reporter. As there were no African-Americans reporting on NASCAR, I was pointing out the obvious, but had a lot of fun pretending to be the character. Many people thought that the Alphonso character was real and did not realize that I was doing Aunt Eloise, Alphonso, and other characters changing back and forth on the radio with ease as I had been doing them for years.

I once interviewed Super Bowl Coach and NASCAR Team Owner Joe Gibbs as Alphonso and the pro he is, he went with it, but the look on his face was priceless. Alphonso would call races such as Martinsville,

The Mart and it drove Big Paul crazy. Michigan became The Mich, Richmond, The Rich, and Wilkesboro, The Wilk. He even made up races such as The Watts in honor of the race riots in the Watts section of Los Angeles.

Alphonso once had a feud with Jimmy Spencer. The feud escalated into a race of John Deere Gators at the North Wilkesboro Speedway called the Last Battle of the Gladiators. This ended up with sponsors supplying the Gators, but there was one problem I was Alphonso and a short, white guy who had too many visits by the Breakfast Club could not be seen racing Spencer on a Gator. Well, Ralph Seagraves got an African-American person named Gene, who worked for R. J. Reynolds pretend to be Alphonso.

During the many years of being a DJ, people accused me of playing "Freebird" too much. Big Paul and I met the survivors of Lynyrd Skynyrd at Daytona. We ended up sitting on top of their bus watching the race.

When Dale Earnhardt won his only Daytona 500, we did not expect him to call in as most drivers did. WTQR was in the hometown R. J. Reynolds Tobacco and he surprised us by calling in from the airplane on his way to New York City to do promotional work. Paul and were amazed at the humble man we heard thanking WTQR, Big Paul and Aunt Eloise for supporting NASCAR. I felt tall that morning realizing what it meant to Dale Earnhardt to have won that race. He later died at the same track and I cannot imagine he would have wanted to go out any other way.

Over the years, I developed a relationship with Earnhardt and Richard Childress, who owned his car. When they were "in the office" at the track, you knew to just leave them alone, but when they were in a playful mood, hanging with them was a lot of fun. Dale called me "The Bitch" He would address Aunt Eloise with "Hey you old bitch."

Old Number 3 was the best. I really believe he could see air and predict how it would affect his racecar. He seemed to sense the aerodynamics of the track and knew where to place his car to take full advantage of it. He could see air.

Earnhardt loved to play practical jokes on Aunt Eloise. One day I found myself talking to Dale and Neil Bonnet. Nearby, there were some Winston Girls, beautiful young ladies who promoted NASCAR for R. J. Reynolds. Dale told me that one of the girls really liked Aunt Eloise and I should go "put The Bitch on her." Well, I walked over, tapped her on the shoulder and began to Aunt Eloise her. She turned around in disgust. It was Jeff Gordon's fiancé and later wife, Brooke Sealey, who walked away as Earnhardt and Bonnet rolled with laughter. I later met Brooke' stepfather, who was a huge Aunt Eloise fan.

You had to be careful with Dale Earnhardt. When he was workin' he was all business. Once he even pulled a knife on me and told me to "Back Off!" You had to pay attention when dealing with him.

I remember once Danny Lawrence, the engine man for Childre Racing, was on the radio so much with Aunt Eloise that Richard got ma and asked him if he wanted to be on the radio or be the engine man. H chose the engines. He once came to our house to visit and my daughte Tabitha came in and said Dale Earnhardt is at the door. It was Danny.

At WTQR, we came up with the Golden Possum Award for the NASCAR champion each year. My brother had a possum taxidermied and stuffed for $200. We gave one to Earnhardt. I asked him what he did with it and he said he hung it in the race shop. The look on Jeff Gordon's face when we presented it to him was classic. We told drive when they called in after winning Sunday race on Monday morning th were now in the running for the Golden Possum Award.

Chapter Sixteen

At WTQR, we discovered that Wachovia Corporate down the street was on the same phone exchange as the station. Whenever we did a call in, bank employees seemed to always be caller twelve. We went to using caller 104 to match the station's frequency 104.1. It took forever to get contest winners.

At the radio station, Aunt Eloise's identity was a closely guarded secret. The doors to the studio were locked at all times during broadcasts, but this did not keep people from coming by to visit. One day Tiny Tim knocked on the door. Paul thought it was a figment of my imagination, but it was really him.

Radio today is a shell of what it was in my heyday. Back then, you could own one AM, one FM, and one TV station. Today, I think you can own four. They are bought up and stripped down. Everything is pre-recorded voice tracking leaving it stagnant. There are only live morning shows and no midday. Usually, there is not even a human being you call at the station after 11 a.m. There is no competition. You might as well as shut the doors. People can listen on apps on their phones or the internet. While this might expand the listenership, I once got a phone call from Switzerland, it takes the human side out of the business, what little business there is left. With music going digital, no one is buying it and the music business is in trouble. Today's kids listen to everything. When I was growing up you listened to one genre.

Country Music comes and goes in waves of crossover artists. Hank Williams started it followed by Patsy Cline and Eddy Arnold singing "Slick Country." Loretta Lynn followed this trend along with Conway Twitty, who saw he could be famous for fifteen minutes as a Pop star, but could have a long career as a Country artist. Glen Campbell and Johnny Cash brought Country back in vogue. Kenny Rogers arrived with a Pop sound, while Randy Travis took it back to old style sound. Garth Brooks and Shania Twain went towards Pop, while George Strait and Alan Jackson went back to a more traditional sound.

I started syndicating Aunt Eloise while in Memphis. You would go to the Country Music Seminar and there might be 100 DJs and Programming Directors at the Andrew Jackson Hotel in Nashville. It was the time of Hayseeds and Big Hair in Country Music when being considered a redneck was a badge of honor and you did not care if people labeled you that way. While there someone would say, "Hey, why don't you come on my show?" Aunt Eloise would call in to other stations on breaks. Once and a while I would fly into to do promos or support fund raising. In Milwaukee, I once did this for a charity for abused kids. In New Orleans, I did stations also owned by Steve Robertson, who owned WTQR. Steve Robertson bought WTQR in 1986, redid the studios and turned some of the personnel over.

Aunt Eloise became a radiotherapist. Whenever a radio host got upset with his co-host, I would get a phone call asking me for motherly advice. Radio partnerships are often about chemistry and when things went astray, I got a phone call.

I got sick of the radio "know it alls", usually Yankees who knew more about our audience than we did. Perception, it is all about perception, and if you do not know your audience, you will fail. Certain types of music will not sell in certain parts of the country. Not everyone cares what happened on *American Idol* or *Dancing With The Stars*. Look at what happened to WTQR after Aunt Eloise left the station.

At one time, I was syndicating Aunt Eloise on twenty other stations including WSM, the home of the Grand Ole Opry. I saved the first check from there. It was four hours every morning, not even getting to sit down, but the checks kept rolling in. Stations in Kinston, North Carolina, Columbia, and even Houston, Texas. I did one nighttime gig in Oklahoma City. I once did five interviews in a row with Lorrie Morgan on five different radio stations. She and I would sneak out in Nashville for Marlboro.

It got to the point that I started turning stations down. I did the syndication myself starting TNT Radio Productions. Sadly, I bet 80% of the people I knew then are not in radio anymore. Every year at Christmas Daddy would ask me, "Son, when are you gonna get a real job?"

Chapter Seventeen

Being a man playing a woman on the radio has a downside. Just like KISS in their makeup days, no one photographed Aunt Eloise without my bonnet, which became the standard apparel for the character. Sometimes it was a long day playing Aunt Eloise. Getting up at 5 a.m. to interview Merle Haggard wearing a dress, bonnet, and brogan shoes tired a fellow out. Sometimes it was uncomfortable, but one time I had an interview with Roy Acuff in his office Roy Acuff Theater in Nashville. On the wall, he had a photo of himself dressed as a woman in a cough medicine advertisement. He told me "Never be ashamed to impersonate a woman. For years, men played women's parts on stage even back in Shakespeare's time." I felt better about playing a female character after hearing that from someone like Roy Acuff. Acuff was impossible to get away from. After an hour, we would excuse ourselves. He told great stories such as the time he taught President Richard Nixon to use a Yo-Yo.

As time went on keeping Aunt Eloise's real identity became more fun than revealing it. In fact, this book will be the first time my identity will come out. Aunt Eloise was referred to as "WW, White and Wide." The character was the ugliest woman and keeping people guessing was always fun. During parades, I would sit behind a cut out with a waving hand and operate the device. Promotional shots filmed me wearing a bonnet and/or a dress. I once did a film that showed Au Eloise wrestling, but when time to reveal me came all you saw was m wearing a black wrestling mask.

Even when celebrities met me, they were shocked. Dolly Part told me she could not believe that voice came of me as she thought I was a good looking man.

A DJ got benefits among these was free meals, deals on cars a even tipping the server was taboo. It did not happen a lot, but it did happen. One of the perks of celebrity, I guess.

I like to get on my soapbox about things in the music industry sometimes. One of these things is taped music that artist use in concerts. I just think they are ripping off people who pay money to se them live. They use auto tune or taped music during their concerts especially acts that dance around and do all these gymnastics. I understand that doing all that one could not possibly be able to sing, but they should let the people know that is what they are doing.

Country Radio Seminar was always in Nashville. It started out with 100 or so DJs, who hung out for a week hanging with the stars, b as country music got bigger, the event went to 300 and then 1,000 DJs and then 1,800. It became so hard to have that close personal contact with the various acts. The event was too big for the stars and it made them uncomfortable. No more passing in the halls. It became many back door meetings you had to sign up for just to get to talk to the stars. It was more business and more professional, but less laid back as it had been in the early days.

Another person I really liked was Tracy Lawrence. He nearly died when first arriving in Nashville when he tried to stop a robbery and was shot three times. One night I was sitting with Tracy Lawrence when he started to sing his new song. The spotlight was shining on me when Tracy started singing. With my fork in my mouth, I was on the big screen as Tracy began to sing "Sticks and Stones."

A person Paul and I did not like was Tim McGraw. He once promised to do an interview with WTQR, blew us off for KTLA, and told us they were a lot bigger than our redneck station. Paul called him an SOB and Aunt Eloise said, "Yeah, what he said." Later we walked out of a McGraw concert and slammed the door loud to make our point.

Paul and I literally traveled all over the world representing WTQR. We went to Olympics in Australia, Japan and Salt Lake City, Utah.

Paul was a nut on these trips. He once walked down the street yelling for Godzilla in Japan.

Aunt Eloise once mounted a campaign for President of the United States. Paul put up signs only to discover there was a woman going around pulling them.

Chapter Eighteen

Big Paul died in a motorcycle accident on his way to Myrtle Beach for bike week on May 16, 2002. His wife, Susan, was on the bike with him and I was told he tried to turn the bike to protect Susan when he realized he was going to be hit. The last thing I told him was "Don't lay that damn thing in the highway. I love you man." I was told the paramedics talked to him as he lay dying and he told them that Jesus was there with him. He was a great guy and my best friend. WXII televised his funeral on local television, but I could not go, as Aunt Eloise was never seen in public. I got on a plane, left town, and found myself in the Florida Keys. I can remember being so upset and my cell phone kept ringing until I just threw it off the Seven Mile Bridge. I came back and went to see Paul's wife at the hospital.

Paul was supplied a bike to ride by Cox Harley Davidson and was suppose to call in that morning at 8:20 a.m. and that became the contentious point that eventually led to my leaving WTQR. Susan filed a worker's compensation claim stating Paul was working that morning. Many at the radio station knew this was the case, but when the company lawyers started pressing the issue, I was the only one that stuck to my guns about it.

Many times as I called in as Aunt Eloise while on vacation. Paul was to do a spot for Cox Harley Davidson. The bike he rode even had a windscreen with a Bruce Hayes ad on it. Well, I testified that Paul was supposed to call in and everyone knew it. During the court proceedings Mark Cox had a billing order with the live call in listed on it. Well, the judge ruled in Susan's favor.

After that, the writing was on the wall at WTQR. I was still under contract for another two years, but the atmosphere changed. People treated me differently. High ups at the station started treating me differently. For instance, the fire alarm at the station sounded like one of those horns on a submarine and many times after a fire drill, I would get on the intercom and say, "Dive, Dive, Dive." I was written up for doing this. That never happened before and it became apparent they were trying to build a case against me to dismiss me before my contract was up.

I heard rumors that I was a drunk, a womanizer, and a liar. I was not going to give up the money and I held my tongue and kept my cool. It was obvious they were going to make my life miserable hoping I would just quit, but I hung on for another four years. My salary was cut but I stayed on after my two year contract ran out. They held a big meeting where this report had all the positive things about my show blacked out, but if you held up to the light just right, you could read it. It stated I was the second most popular Piedmont Triad personality. They were trying to get me to lose my temper, but I kept my cool.

After Big Paul died, I went to the CMA Awards in November. It was my first time in Nashville without Big Paul and it felt strange. That year Toby Keith was up for six awards and did not win a single one. There were stories about Toby being upset and walking out of the show, but I want to tell a story about the kind of man Toby is. The next night after the show, I was at Palms Restaurant and so was Toby. One of his people approached me and said that Toby wanted to see me. Well, I went back to a private room where Toby put his arm around me and said" I wanna tell you what a great dude Big Paul was." Toby and Paul were friends due to a joint interest in horses, which they talked about often. During this time two women from Bill Dotson's hometown wanted Toby's autograph and he said bring them on over. His whole attitude that night was of a decent man. Now, for a man being accused of being a diva after not winning six awards to take the time to tell me that about Paul and to sign a couple of autographs meant a lot to me and told me he was not the self-absorbed man the rumors were saying.

Sometimes you do not realize the effect you have on other people's lives. Joe Nichols grew up in Arkansas listening to me on the radio out of Memphis. Joe had five number one singles on country radio. He told someone he wanted to meet Aunt Eloise. He hugged me and said he had listened to me his whole life and he could not tell me how many mornings he went to work laughing listening to Aunt Eloise.

For 23 years, it was worth the change. I was paid so much money before it all ended at WTQR. Now the government got half of that, but it still was more money than I ever dreamed. Fifty years old and I was John Wayne, but even the Duke had his horse shot out from under him and so did I. Big Paul was gone and Bill Dotson, my old partner in Memphis came and joined me, but that was when Dr. Death came knocking.

I was having pains in my stomach, but did not go to a doctor and one day at home I just collapsed. The ambulance came and on my way to the hospital, I almost died from diverticulitis. My intestines ruptured and while taking me to another hospital, I almost died again. Doctors called my family because they thought I was gone. I survived because I had some great doctors, but on top of that, I could not walk. Two hip operations and I spent more time in the hospital than an x-ray machine.

Three years of in and out of the hospital, a Colostomy bag for a year and I was ready to give up. Dan Sykes, the radio station engineer, hooked up a at home radio thing, where I could broadcast from home on my back. I cannot even think what that might have sounded like to my listeners and I would cry after every show thinking who wants to listen to this crap.

Earlier I mentioned that twice in my life, I nearly died twice. In Memphis, in a balloon and a helicopter accidents and in Winston-Salem after surgery. They called me Code Blue Toby due to my brushes with death. The nurses told Tammy that I also did radio shows in my sleep. As I spent thirty days in the hospital, they came to hear all the characters including Aunt Eloise and Alphonso.

Days and weeks went by and I was so scared the people would forget me and by the time I healed the people would be gone. I thought radio as I knew it would change, and nobody would be listening to me. Well, I got well enough for my wife to drive me to work, colostomy bag and all, but another hip was going bad and back in the hospital I went. Feeling sorry for myself, I just got to where I wanted God to take me. I cannot live like this.

I got a letter from a 12-year-old girl, who also had a colostomy bag, but just one difference, her's was for life. That letter and her story made me feel ashamed. Here I was going to go back to normal and this girl had to live with hers for life. I stopped feeling sorry for myself that day and all I could focus on was doing what I had to do to get well. I lost my best friend and then I went and had all this happen and after I got well, the station cut me lose. What else was God going to do with me next?

My last interview at WTQR was an up and coming female artist who wrote her own material. Bobby Young represented her and was a old friend. Bill Dotson was ready to go to home, but I got him to do it. This skinny teenager came into the studio. She said her Father had something to do with the Orange Bowl and played some of her songs. My last interview was with Taylor Swift.

When the end finally came at WTQR, I had a 15.2 share of the radio audience. It had been as high as 26% of the market, both huge numbers by today's standards in radio. In October 2008, a new General Manager came to WTQR and after twenty-three years, I was unemployed. The economy tanked and it took us two years to sell our house in Advance.

I could not work for six months because of my contract and it might have put me back in the hospital. Nobody returned my calls for a job.

Of course, at this time only three companies owned all the stations. That is like only having three burger joints because by law you cannot own a burger joint unless the government says you can. The rich got richer, three thousand radio jobs were lost because of the monopoly, and the lobbyist won. Competition is the key, but radio became the playground of a few. After twenty years, most people get a gold watch and a pension. I got neither.

Aunt Eloise's morning cohort, Andy Wright at WBRF.

Chapter Nineteen

The snow, ah the snow. I always loved to see it snow, but now I cringe when it comes. Coming from the sand hills of South Carolina, snow was a wonderful thing because it might snow once every five years. One inch shut down the roads and the men went hunting. The kids tried to build snowmen because schools would close. Momma made homemade soup. I only saw one good snow or ice storm that hit home when I was about fifteen. A freak of a storm that had pine tree limbs busting left and right like shotguns going off at a skeet shoot. Fifteen years later in Memphis, I saw 26 inches hit the ground. Five years here on the mountain, it has snowed every year. The snow has stayed on the ground for months at a time. Average is about twelve inches each year. Snow should come on Friday after work and be gone before work on Monday.

Radio as I knew it is over. The new age has overcome me and I am at the buggy whip stage. So where do you go from here? Good Question. I always wanted to be a writer, but books will be outdated too, I think. I will end this book with these thoughts.

I first started with political soapbox on the air while in Columbia. I went after State Senator Floyd Spence, who had a sweetheart deal with South Carolina Electric and Gas. The General Manager called me into his office to explain where I got my informatio I told the Senator and my boss, I read it in *The State* newspaper. It was that no one thought about talking about politics on the radio before ar making fun of the politicians.

When I got to Memphis, just a few miles upstream was Cape Girardeau, Missouri, where Rush Limbaugh grew up. Did he hear me talking politics? I do not know, but he sure did change radio. The Mayc of Memphis first act after election was to buy a Cadillac. Jimmy Carter had us in lines to get gas and this dude is driving a Cadillac. There was Governor of Tennessee selling pardons that resulted in a song "Pardor Me Ray."

I have seen so many changes in this career. When I started yo aunt was an overweight lady who was married to the same man for o thirty years, with the slight hint of a mustache, who wore glasses, cooked with an apron, loved you to death, always sent you a birthday card, and had that certain smell when she hugged you so hard you thought you would bust. Today, your aunt is a twice divorced, still smoking hot, and is probably a cougar

The last five years (2009-2014) working for Debbie Epperson Stringer at WBRF, Classic Country 98.1, with Andy Wright have been a great adventure, no doubt. Things are on a looser ladder than the ones I have climbed in my early days in radio. The pressure is gone and the drive to be number one is not even in question. I can say with all honesty that it has taken the last five years to come to grip with it all. I am like a football coach who won on every level of the game, but now the owner and alumni are not at my throat about winning. Just play the game.

So, why did the possum cross the road? Ever notice how few possums make it across the road? Well, this possum made it across the road. Radio gave my family a great life, meeting great people, some even legends. I have no great philosophical message. I had a good time and lived a good life. This is my story and I am sticking to it.

A Possum Photo Album

Above, Robert Thomas "Toby" Young with Vanna White. Below, Toby having fun with Conway Twitty.

"Toby" with Bill Anderson

Toby with Vince Gill.

Toby with "Sweetness," Walter Payton of the Chicago Bears.

Above, Toby with NASCAR driver, Jeff Gordon. Below, Toby blowing o daughter Tabitha's birthday candles.

Toby with Big Paul during the WTQR years with Dale Earnhardt, who always called Toby aka Aunt Eloise, "The Bitch." Below, Toby with NASCAR driver Cale Yarborough.

Above, Toby with Randy Owens of Alabama. Below, Big Paul, Jay B. Brown, Randy Owens and Toby.

Aunt Eloise's only hit "Robbin' You" about Memphis Light, Gas, and Power.

Nothing Toby enjoys more than Clemson football.

Toby with Clemson football player Perry Tuttle, who caught the winning pass at the 1981 National Championship against Nebraska and was on the cover of Sports Illustrated.

Above, Toby with NASCAR driver Ernie Irvin. Below with Big Paul at the Olympics in Nagano, Japan, in 1998.

*Sosserman Entertainment
& Waterpark Complex...
Home of Beautiful Lake Sosserman*

Press Release

George Sosserman, President and CEO of the above named company announced today the replacement of the beloved Howard Nemenz is The Honorable Mr. Robert T. Young of Advance North Carolina. Mr. Young will assume the duties of Vice-President & General Manager of this company on March 1. Sosserman stated that he based his decision on the aggressive campaign and versatile nature of Mr. Young's platform. When contacted Mr. Young could not respond!!!!!!!!!

Learn to love him

Toby having fun with Howard Nemenz and George Sosserman at WTQR.

THIRTY·FIRST CMA AWARDS

Wednesday, September 24
8 p.m. Eastern
CBS

September 8, 1997

Toby "Aunt Eloise" Young
WTQR
PO Box 3018
Winston-Salem, NC 27102

Dear Toby:

Congratulations once again on being named Large Market Broadcast Personality Of The Year! I wanted to give you some additional information on what to expect on your big night.

A variety of awards will be presented during a Pre-Telecast Awards ceremony, including the Broadcast Awards. The presentations will begin promptly at 6:30. You will need to be in your seats no later than 6:15. What will happen during this awards presentation is as follows: your name will be called as the recipient of the Large Market Broadcast Personality Of The Year. For productions purposes, you will proceed to go on stage and accept a Crystal Trophy, along with the other winners. However, keep in mind that this is not the actual award you will take home. To receive YOUR Crystal Trophy go to "house right" (facing the stage, it is the area directly to your right) immediately following the telecast (approx. 10 PM). I will be waiting for you there to distribute the awards accordingly.

The CMA Crystal Trophy is made of hand blown crystal. Each is one of a kind. Because of the value of these awards we felt it was imperative that you pick up your award after the show. This is to avoid you having to hold and possibly drop (oops...I'd hate for that to happen!!) the award during the telecast.

Feel free to give me a call if you have any questions at all. I look forward to meeting you all and congratulating you in person on September 24th. See you there!!

Sincerely,

Lara Henley
Membership Development Representative

ONE MUSIC CIRCLE SOUTH, NASHVILLE, TN 37203 • (615)244-2840 • FAX (615)242-4784 • WWW.COUNTRYMUSIC.ORG

Memphis Press-Scimitar   Saturday, December 4, 1982   **23**

Try 'possum chili as Christmas feast

JUST TROLLING:

Can you believe it? Aunt Eloise Louise, local radio personality, hasn't got a 'possum chili recipe. And Aunt Eloise Louise knows about 'possums — fried, boiled, baked, you name it, Aunt Eloise knows, except for 'possum chili.

Buck Patton

However, just in time for Christmas dinners everywhere, and especially for Aunt Eloise Louise, I have found a genuine imitation Cajun 'possum chili recipe — at Tommy Thomson's Western Lounge. It goes very well with western boots and can be a very hot item on Christmas Day.

Here, outdoor fans, is the recipe:

    2 pounds ground 'possum meat
    ½ cup beef suet
    2 cans kidney beans
    2 cans (8 oz.) tomato sauce
    3 to 5 tbsp chili powder
    2 shakes cayenne pepper
    5 shakes of red pepper if you really want to liven things up
    ½ tsp garlic powder
    ½ tsp crushed oregano
    ½ tsp salt
    ⅓ cup water, optional

Brown 'possum in suet. Add remaining ingredients, except beans. Simmer for 1½ hours, adding additional water when necessary. Stir occasionally. If mixture becomes too thick add enough water for desired thickness. Add beans 20 minutes before chili is done. (If 'possum is not available venison will do, but don't tell Aunt Eloise Louise.) Serves eight not-too-hungry folks.

A Fun Parade Is Part; Advance Knows What Christmas Is All About

By Mike Barnhardt
Davie County Enterprise Record

ADVANCE - On Christmas Eve, Santa Claus will climb aboard a fire truck here and make some special rounds - visiting the elderly, the young and shut-ins. He'll take them gifts and plenty of holiday happiness.

It's what Christmas is all about.

Around these parts, it's also a lot of fun.

Area residents are invited to join in that fun at 10 a.m. Saturday when the third annual Advance Christmas Parade takes place. It starts on Cornatzer Road at the school, heads south at N.C. 801 and ends on Peoples Creek Road.

More than 200 entries have already signed up, with many more expected. Want to take part? Show up on Saturday morning and they'll line your entry up with the others. There's no entry fee. Be tasteful, but have some fun.

"Our deadline is Saturday at 10," said organizer Linda Carter, the unofficial sheriff of Advance. "If you ain't here at 10 o'clock, you ain't in our parade."

Among the early entries are the mayors of Advance, Hillsdale and Bixby. The Advance mayor will demonstrate a new liquor still recently made for that "high" office. Don't try to put him in jail, because he's already been in "Jale," erected next to L&S Grocery. Several area residents have been put in that jale, and approximately $2,000 in

Please See Advance – Page 4

must do the lovefeast and candle service on Christmas eve.

A United Methodist minister confided once that he was happy to give Christmas to the Moravians. He encouraged all his parishioners to go to the Moravian service ... with him.

He was happy for the night off.

Besides, Moravians do Christmas well. The lovefeast. The beeswax candle. The bun and coffee all symbolize the important things about Christmas — things that we forget at the mall or in the hubbub of shopping and decorating.

It's really amazing how Christmas has grown beyond its humble beginning. Christmas isn't even the focal point of the Christian church. Easter is.

But Christmas has become a commercial bonanza, part of what drives the economy of the nation.

Christmas sales make or break many companies.

I'm always amazed at the energy some people have for celebrating Christmas. I marvel at the houses that are strung with thousands of lights — little Tanglewoods. Those people risk life and limb to climb ladders to outline their roof and windows with Christmas lights.

I'm convinced they don't watch television. They have more free time — and nerve — than I have.

But how should we spend Christmas?

In truth, watching children stumble over their lines in the Christmas pageant evokes all the memories of when we did the same thing. It's a wonderful experience to drive to the mountains for a tree. Christmas cards are a wonderful way to reach out to friends you haven't heard from in a year. And Tanglewood and the Moravian lovefeast are good times to be with the family.

Maybe we worry too much about the "spirit of Christmas." Maybe we are too concerned about making this be best Christ-

Above and below, Toby and Big Paul in Japan at Nagano Olympics in 1998. Coca-Cola sent radio representatives from each of the 50 states

Earl Thomas Connelly at the WTQR Family Reunion.

Above, Carl Perkins with Toby, his father, mother, wife, Tammy, and t Becks in Memphis, Tennessee. Below, Toby having fun with daughte Tara at Halloween.

Above, Big Paul in Japan and below the airplane ride home.

Above, T-Tommy, owner of the steak house in Memphis, Tennessee where Elvis loved to come have a steak, shown on the next page Elvis favorite booth. Below, young Toby Young.

Toby as the world's worst Elvis impersonator, Bo Bo Boatwright.

Pam Tillis.

Faith Hill.

Martina McBride.

Tracy Lawrence.

Above, Juice Newton, and below, John Michael Montgomery.

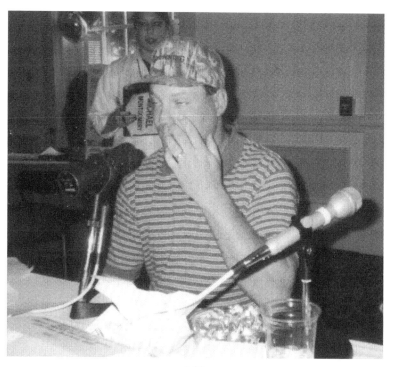

Above, Johnny and June Carter Cash. Below, RCA Records Rep Wayne Edwards with recording artist Sylvia, who had a hit with "Nobody" and "Drifter."

Eddie Rabbit and salesperson, Patty Scott at WTQR Family Reunion.

Big Paul in Japan at Nagano 1998 Olympics.

T. G. Sheppard at WTQR Family Reunion. Below, Toby and Big Paul in Nashville, Tennessee.

Toby with songwriter, Randy Boudreaux, in Nashville, Tennessee.

Toby at WCOS in Columbia, South Carolina, with Ken Martin and some of the sales staff.

Above, Toby at WTQR Family Reunion with Sonny Neal, son of Bobb Neal, Elvis's first manager with Patty Scott on the left. Below, Toby with Glenda and Les Acree.

Toby with daughter, Tara.

Above, Toby's father, James H. Young. Below Toby and Tammy's daughter, Tabitha at Clemson.

Toby and Big Paul in Japan for 1998 Nagano Olympics.

Toby and Tammy's daughters Tara, Tabitha, with Cousin April.

Toby's old friend, Flossie Johnson, the first lady of NASCAR.

Above, Toby with Joe Nichols. Below, Tanya Tucker.

Above, Toby with Ralph Seagraves, the man who brought NASCAR and RJ Reynolds together. Below, WTQR staff at Family Reunion concert.

Gene Overby of WSJS.

Dale and Teresa Earnhardt with Ardell and Ralph Seagraves.

The "Possum Cave" wall denoting a lifetime of radio success.

Bob Costner

Smith Patterson

Cotton Plantation built in 1820s. Below, Family Reunion in the 1920

Katie Mackie, mother of Louise Taylor.

The Youngs: Jimmie, Elsie, James H., Beverly, Clara, Daisy, Mary, an Ann.

The Taylors: A. B. Louise, Bobby and Frieda.

Grandma and Grandpa Cotton, David and Clara.

Toby's grandmothers on whom Aunt Eloise is based. Elise Cotton on the right and Louise Taylor on the left.

The transistor radio from WCOS that started a career in radio and the CMA Award that was the ultimate prize.

Above, today at WBRF, Toby and Andy Wright handle the morning show. Below, WTQR days with Danny Hall, Melody Dean Smith and Dale Mitchell.

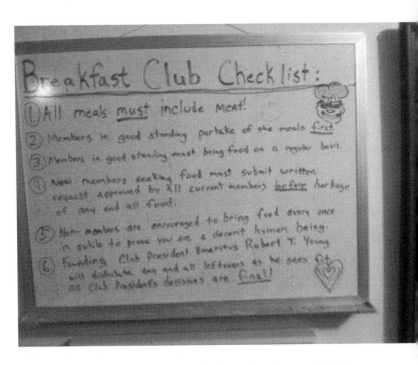

Breakfast Club Rules from the days at WTQR.

A Few Words From The Ghost Writer In The Sky

"Is she really a woman?" That is the question everyone asked when I told them about working on this book. My answer was always the same. "He/She/It is the ugliest woman I ever saw."

He is one of the funniest human beings I have had the pleasure to know. I can remember listening to Aunt Eloise on WTQR when he/she/it was in the heyday of his/her/its career. I was not a country music fan, but I still thought Aunt Eloise was funny and I still do.

While assisting on this book, I spent many hours listening to Robert Thomas "Toby" Young tell stories about his decades on the radio as one of the most popular DJs in the history of country radio. We consumed many plates of barbecue at The Smokehouse in Galax, Virginia, after his morning show on WBRF 98.1 FM. We talked as we consumed many gallons of sweet tea as "Toby" told me about his life sitting under a painting of Robert E. Lee at the Battle of Sailor's Creek in April 1865.

This leads to another story about the surrender a few days later of Robert E. Lee to U. S. Grant at Appomattox Court House on April 9, 1865. History via Aunt Eloise goes something like this. Robert E. Lee says to U. S. Grant. "Okay Ulysses. Let us make a deal. We can end this war if you promise to send all your friends down to Myrtle Beach every summer for two weeks to spend their money and help rebuild the Southern economy." Grant replies, "That sounds like a good deal to me." Lee responds. "But if they stay more than two weeks, Ulysses, th[ey] will be Damn Yankees."

There was the story about Aunt Eloise finding him, her, itself, the Outrigger Bar in New Orleans, Louisiana. After playing a few game[s] of pinball Toby found himself at the bar talking with a woman, who w[as] a man, resulting in a fast cab ride back to the hotel alone before Toby found out what the role reversal of men dressing as woman was all about.

There was a discussion of the UNC vs. Clemson basketball series, where Clemson has never won a game in Chapel Hill, North Carolina. Eloise's theory is simple. When you walk into the Dean Dom[e] and see that banner hanging up in honor of ACC Referee Lenny Wirtz [it] is easy to understand why Clemson could never win a game where ei[ght] played five Clemson Tigers. (Five UNC players and three referees.) Th[ere] is no banner honoring any referee, but the joke for those of us who g[et] it, is that the corruption now present at the oldest state university is nothing new, just not exposed as it has been over the last few years.

So, why did the possum cross the road? Was it to show a South Carolina Gamecock it could be done? No, this possum crossed the road to find a turkey (I am a Virginia Tech alumni and our mascot is a turkey.) to help him, her, it, write a book about living his dream of being on the radio as his grandfather first exposed him to in South Carolina. When you spend time with an icon of Southern culture, you realize many truths about the region where you live.

Spending your life making people laugh as Toby has done is not a bad way to make a living. It has been my great pleasure to get to know and spend time with Robert Thomas "Toby" Young, Aunt Eloise Louise Cotton, and I hope you enjoy his, her, its story.

--Thomas D. Perry, November 23, 2014, somewhere in the suburbs of Mayberry RFD.

Ressie Star Young.
October 2001-March 2, 2014.

Acknowledgements

Thanks to my grandmothers, Elise and Louise, for giving me Aunt Eloise. I met my wife, Tammy, at WCOS in 1979. We are now married for thirty-six years. How she put up with me I will never know, but she is my angel. She has given me two beautiful daughters, Tara and Tabitha. All these women have touched my life and have always believed in me and been there for me no matter what. I love you all and thank you.

Thank to my brother Bo, who always looked after me and my other brother, Danny. I was 12 years old before I realized that my name was not "BO DANNY DAMN IT TOBY".

Thanks to my "Ghost Writer," Tom Perry. Thanks Jennifer Gregory, Debbie Hall, and Amy Snyder for proof reading this book. Thanks to God for putting up with me.

Index

A

Acree, 2, 49, 52, 77, 78, 90, 92
Acuff, 121
Adams, 33, 63, 76
Advance, 101, 130
Aikman, 59
Alabama, 47, 48, 65, 74, 142
Alphonso Willingham, 113
American Idol, 100, 119
ARK Studios, 78
Arkansas, 73, 128
Arnold, 118
Aunt Eloise, 2, 5, 7, 10, 11, 25, 34, 37, 40, 43, 49, 51, 52, 61, 62, 65, 73, 76, 86, 87, 100, 101, 103, 104, 105, 107, 108, 109, 113, 115, 117, 118, 119, 121, 123, 124, 125, 126, 128, 129, 141, 191, 192, 193, 195

B

Baker, 67
Battle of the Waffle House, 55, 65
Beale Street, 61, 76
Beatles, 63
Bertram, 68
Big Daddy's Saloon, 34
Big Paul, 105, 106, 107, 108, 114, 115, 125, 127, 128, 141, 152, 155, 166, 167
Bill Black Combo, 63, 64
Black, 25, 28, 29, 63, 64, 78, 82, 85, 113
Blevins, 90
Blues Alley, 61
Blues Brothers Band, 55
Bo Bo Boatwright, 63, 81
Bogan, 43
Bombay Bicycle Club, 62
Bonnet, 115
Boogie Man, 29
Borgnine, 85
Bowery, 47
Bradshaw, 59
Breakfast Club, 103, 104, 114
Brooks, 64, 94, 108, 118
Brown, 85, 86, 104
Bryant, 74
Buck, 90, 91, 103
Buffet, 33, 64
Burke, 77
Burton, 63, 105
Bush, 50

C

Campbell, 118
Carol Burnett Show, 101
Carter, 134, 164
Cash, 54, 77, 82, 118, 164
Cassius Clay, 76
Castaways, 32, 33, 47, 81
Cayman Islands, 59
Chambers, 98
Charleston, 24
Charlotte, 97, 99, 101, 103
Childress, 115
Clemson, 22, 30, 33, 59, 89, 90, 92, 112, 144, 192
Cline, 59, 85, 118
CMA, 49, 107, 127
Collins, 67
Columbia, 11, 12, 13, 22, 23, 29, 30, 33, 34, 39, 40, 41, 42, 47, 51, 52, 58, 61, 81, 90, 100, 103, 109, 111, 119, 133, 169

Conley, 55, 94
Connelly, 77, 153
Conway, 77, 101, 118, 137
Cook, 47
Coolidge, 63
Corbin, 81
Corman, 101
Cosell, 61
Cotton, 10, 11, 12, 24, 51, 193
Country Radio Seminar, 91, 122
Cox Harley Davidson, 125, 126
Crosby, 60

D

Dallas Cowboys, 59
Dancing With The Stars, 100, 119
Daniels, 55, 86, 108
Darlington, 22, 99
David Lettermen Show, 57
Dees, 51, 76
Dennis, 51, 52, 87
Donahue, 84
Dotson, 61, 62, 74, 127, 128, 130
Drifters, 34
Dukes of Hazard, 100

E

Eagles, 60, 74
Earnhardt, 105, 114, 115, 116, 141
Ed Sullivan Show, 77
Edwards, 48, 49, 50
Electric Weenie, 76
Elvis, 53, 54, 63, 65, 68, 69, 70, 74, 77, 81, 82, 85, 94, 108, 156, 158
Emery, 97
Evans, 68

F

Farmer, 106

Federal Communication Commission 36
Flair,, 57
Flint, 105
Four Tops, 28
Foxx, 61
France, 95, 105
Frye, 60
Fuller, 103

G

Garner, 13, 112
Gentry, 47
GHB Broadcasting, 43
Gibbs, 113
Gill, 60, 138
Goldwater, 22
Gordon, 116, 140
Graceland, 51, 53, 81, 82
Grant, 41, 42, 191
Green, 68, 74, 77
Griffith, 30, 81, 100, 101
Gunsmoke, 101

H

Haggard, 67, 121
Hall, 55, 61, 91, 103
Hardees, 39, 104
Hayes, 126
Henley, 60
Herndon, 47
Herring, 29, 37, 42
Hope, 84
Howard, 59, 60, 61, 62, 89, 103, 14
Huey's, 73

I

IPTAY, 89

J

Jackson, 64, 108, 118
Jennings, 82
Johnson, 97, 112
Jordan, 49, 64
Juicy Fruit, 95

K

Kaufman, 57
Keith, 127
Kelly, 48, 75
Kenney Roger's Hideaway, 63, 73
King, 54, 57, 58, 63, 78, 81, 85
KISS, 121
Kline, 54
Knotts, 101
Krispy Kreme, 103
Kristofferson, 63
Kristopherson, 82

L

Lancaster, 73
Last Battle of the Gladiators, 114
Lawler, 57
Lawrence, 123, 162
Leadon, 60
Level, 95
Leveler, 85
Lewis, 68, 73
Limbaugh, 134
Los Angeles Coliseum, 76
Louie's Backyard, 64
Lynn, 54, 60, 118
Lynyrd Skynyrd, 114

M

Mahoney, 67
Martin, 51, 52, 78, 169
Martindale, 2
Martinsville, 113
Maryland Fried Chicken, 75
Mayberry, 100, 193
MCA, 64
McGraw, 123
Memphis, 2, 3, 49, 51, 52, 53, 54, 55, 57, 58, 59, 61, 62, 63, 64, 65, 67, 68, 71, 73, 74, 76, 77, 78, 81, 84, 85, 86, 87, 89, 90, 92, 94, 118, 128, 129, 133, 134, 154, 156
Memphis Showboats, 74
Memphis State University, 63
Mercury Records, 95
Mid-South Wrestling, 57
Mississippi River, 62, 73
Mitchell, 92, 98, 99, 103
Moorer, 52
Morgan, 119
Mount Airy, 100
Mustang, 30
Myrtle Beach, 12, 32, 41, 47, 48, 60, 61, 81, 125, 192

N

NASCAR, 97, 98, 99, 105, 106, 108, 113, 115, 140, 141
Nashville, 35, 50, 59, 73, 86, 91, 93, 94, 95, 103, 118, 120, 121, 122, 123, 127, 167, 168
Neil, 63, 81, 115
Nelson, 64, 82
Neman, 103
New York Yankees, 97
Newman, 106
Nixon, 121
No Time For Sergeants, 30
North Wilkesboro, 97, 99, 114
Nugent, 60

O

O'Neal, 30
Olympics, 76, 123
Opryland, 86, 108
Orange Bowl, 90, 130
Osborne, 76
Overby, 111
Owen, 47

P

Packers, 74
Parker, 69, 71
Parton, 55, 64, 122
Patterson, 104
Pavilion, 47
Perkins, 54, 77, 154
Perry, 5, 6, 8, 193, 195
Petty, 105, 106
Peyton, 60
Phillips, 2, 65, 82
Pittsburgh Steelers, 59
Plummer, 41, 42
possum, 8, 25, 34, 61, 87, 193
Presley, 53, 69, 82
Prestojokomo, 57
Pride, 49, 112
Prine, 68
Pulliams, 105
Pure Prairie League, 60
Pusser, 67

R

Rainbow Catering, 105
Ray, 78, 134
RCA, 48, 49, 69, 82
Red Fern, 29
Redding, 77
Rendezvous, 61
Reynolds, 98, 99, 108, 112, 114, 115

Rich, 68, 114
Richland, 12, 28
Robertson, 98, 119
Rockingham, 99
Rodgers, 118
Rogers, 3, 63, 64, 68, 74
Ronstadt, 60
Roper, 100

S

Schmidt, 60
Scirca, 104
Scott, 29, 111, 165
Seagraves, 97, 98, 108, 109, 114
Sealey, 116
Shakespeare, 121
Sherman, 11
Sister Rose, 34
Slaughter, 97
Smith, 7, 104, 112
South Carolina Electric and Gas, 23, 134
Spence, 133
St. Jude, 84
Starlight Drive In, 81
Starr, 54
Stone Cold, 57
Straight, 81, 118
Strait, 54
Sun Studios, 82
Swift, 130
Sykes, 129

T

Tams, 34
Tanner, 84
Taylor, 12, 22, 130
The Hulk, 57
The State, 134

Thomas, 5, 6, 8, 54, 55, 78, 84, 94, 96, 137, 153, 191, 193
Thunderbird Lounge, 33
Tiny Tim, 117
TNT Radio Productions, 120
Tom T. Hall, 55, 61
Travis, 54, 118
T-Tommy, 61, 67, 68, 69, 70, 156
Tucker, 63, 84
Turbeville, 31
Twain, 118
Twilight Lounge, 33
Twitty, 77, 118, 137

U

UNC, 111, 192
Unitas, 75
University of South Carolina, 32, 90

V

Vantage Championships, 112
Victory Junction Gang, 106
Virginia Tech, 193

W

Wake Forest, 111, 112
Walker, 55, 64
Wallace, 105
Wayne, 48, 49, 50, 67, 84, 98, 128
WBRF, 191
WCAY, 34, 35

WCOS, 29, 31, 32, 33, 35, 37, 39, 40, 47, 51, 90, 169, 195
WDIA, 78
Webster, 91, 103
West, 34, 55, 64, 85
White, 25, 60, 74, 78, 82, 121, 137
Wild Wendy, 104
Williams, 93, 118
Winston Cup, 98, 108
Winston-Salem, 59, 60, 89, 90, 92, 103, 108, 111, 129
Wirtz, 192
WIVK, 92
WMC, 2, 49, 52, 53, 57, 83, 92
Wood, 74
Woods, 63
WSJS, 111
WSM, 119
WSOC, 99, 103
WTQR, 63, 89, 90, 92, 94, 97, 98, 100, 101, 103, 105, 111, 112, 114, 117, 119, 123, 125, 126, 128, 130, 141, 147, 153, 165, 167, 191
Wynette, 67

Y

Young, 5, 6, 8, 10, 12, 24, 87, 101, 109, 130, 137, 191, 193, 194

Z

Zimmerson, 33
ZZ Top, 79

For Further Reading

Visit Tom Perry's Laurel Hill Publishing LLC

www.freestateofpatrick.com

Made in the USA
Charleston, SC
27 November 2014